LIGHTKEEPING ON THE ST. LAWRENCE

NORMAND LAFRENIÈRE

LIGHTKEEPING ON THE ST. LAWRENCE

THE END OF AN ERA

NORMAND LAFRENIÈRE

DUNDURN PRESS

TORONTO & OXFORD

Published by Dundurn Press Limited in cooperation with the Department of Canadian Heritage and the Canada Communication Group – Publishing, Supply and Services Canada.

Catalogue number: R62-287-1995E

Editing: Judith Turnbull
Design: Sebastian Vasile
Production: Métrolitho

Canadian Cataloguing in Publication Data
Lafrenière, Normand
    Lightkeeping on the St. Lawrence

Issued also in French under title:
    Gardien de phare dans le Saint-Laurent
Includes bibliographical references.
ISBN 1-55002-277-6

1. Lighthouses – Saint-Lawrence River – History. 2. Lighthouses – Saint-Lawrence, Gulf of – History. 3. Lighthouse keepers – Saint-Lawrence River – History. 4. Lighthouse keepers – Saint-Lawrence, Gulf of – History I. Title.

VK1027 .S35L3413 1996   387.1'55'09714   C96–930351–3

Dundurn Press Limited
2181 Queen Street East
Suite 301
Toronto, Canada
M4E 1E5

Dundurn Distribution
73 Lime Walk
Headington, Oxford
England
0X3 7AD

Dundurn Press Limited
1823 Maryland Avenue
P.O. Box 1000
Niagara Falls, N.Y.
U.S.A. 14302-1000

CONTENTS

ACKNOWLEDGEMENTS

A number of people assisted in making this study of lightkeeping possible. I would therefore like to express my sincere appreciation to them here. My thanks go first to Gisèle Bernier and to André Bonneau of the Archives of the Port of Quebec for their judicious advice and warm welcome. I would also like to thank Canadian Coast Guard personnel, and in particular Gilles Savard, Lise Cloutier, Jean-Pierre Bégin, Gilles Richard and Denis Chamard for their indispensable technical support.

And lastly, I would like to draw attention to the very special contribution made by thirty former lighthouse keepers whose names appear at the end of this study. My most sincere thanks go out to these people. This book is dedicated to each and every one of them.

INTRODUCTION

This study of lightkeeping lies within the scope of various initiatives being undertaken by Parks Canada to develop the lighthouses at Pointe au Père, Cap de Bon-Désir, Cap Gaspé and the Pointe Noire Range. It is intended to provide a general overview of lightkeeping since its emergence in 1809 in Quebec (then called Lower Canada) until its disappearance from this same area in 1988 with the automation of light stations.

The archives of the Trinity House of Quebec have made it possible to retrace the first milestones in lightkeeping in this province during the nineteenth century. As the ancestor of Transport Canada, the Trinity House of Quebec had full jurisdiction over all issues relating to aids to navigation and to pilotage on the St. Lawrence River between 1805 and 1869. This important archival depository, which covers the period 1805 to 1875, contains a wealth of information such as correspondence exchanged between the first lighthouse keepers and the administrators of the Trinity House of Quebec. The vast majority of the information on the first lightkeepers' working conditions and ways of life was therefore obtained through a multitude of strictly administrative documents.

As for the twentieth century, I met with thirty former lightkeepers who worked along the Gaspé, Lower St. Lawrence, Saguenay and North Shore. The sample group was highly representative including as it did 75 percent of the last surviving lightkeepers in Quebec. The data collected from the keepers also cover most of the light stations, as the majority of the men worked at more than one St. Lawrence light. Furthermore, because a significant number learned lightkeeping from their fathers, when their various accounts are combined they cover the greater part of the twentieth century.

Administration of the St. Lawrence lighthouses was the responsibility of the Department of Marine and Fisheries between 1870 and 1935; since 1936, Transport Canada (Canadian Coast Guard) has fulfilled this role.

Chapter One

A RIVER TO BE TAMED

UNDER FRENCH RULE

Natural Hazards

Since their discovery by the first explorers, the St. Lawrence River and its Gulf have presented ocean-going mariners with some of the most difficult sailing conditions in the world. Even today, navigation in this waterway is subject to the caprices of its many natural obstacles, including reefs and shoals, currents and tides, fog and sandbanks.

The archives of the French regime contain many voyagers' accounts that describe the hazards – indeed perils – of sailing on the river below Quebec City. Even towards the end of French rule, after the waterway had been used for a century and a half, the conditions appear to have improved very little. At least this is the impression given by the soldier and mariner Louis Antoine de Bougainville in his assessment of 1756: "The reefs which are found in such great number in this river and the most dangerous and exacting navigation of its waters constitute Quebec's greatest defence."[1]

Such leaders in the maritime world as Gabriel Pellegrin, pilot and Quebec harbourmaster in 1751, agreed wholeheartedly with Bougainville. In his 1757 report on navigation in Canada, Pellegrin recounts that "navigating in Canada has been regarded as fraught with difficulties, as indeed it is; but it is not merely the fog that makes it thus; the very real hazards such as shallows, isles and dangerous shoals do not appear until well into the river."[2] Pellegrin points out the section that poses a significant hazard to mariners as they enter the Gulf from Newfoundland: "From the Grand Banks to Bic requires practical experience that can only be acquired through a number of years of navigation and singular attentiveness so as to be able to recognize the depths of the various shoals that must be negotiated, and their respective size and distance."[3]

---

[1] "Journal de Bougainville," in *RAPQ, 1923–1924* (Quebec: L.-A. Proulx, 1924), 310 (translation).
[2] Gabriel Pellegrin, "Mémoire sur la navigation du Canada," 1757, in *RCCA, 1905* (Ottawa: S.E. Dawson, 1905), Part 5, 3.
[3] Ibid., 3 (translation).

Hydrographic Surveys

Although pilots were required to use extreme caution, local and French authorities did attempt to improve navigation between Newfoundland's "Grand Banks" and Quebec City. Between 1727 and 1740, for example, an ambitious program of hydrographic surveys got under way with the appointment of Richard Testu de La Richardière to the position of port captain of Quebec. La Richardière explored the north and south shores of the river, the Strait of Belle Isle, Île Saint-Jean (now Prince Edward Island), Chaleur Bay and the Strait of Canso.[4] At the same time, other pilots, such as Jean Deshaies and the king's pilots specially dispatched to Quebec City to help in the surveys, recorded an entire series of observations and made up drawings that were then transferred to charts by geographers at the naval map office.

Pilot Training

Well before the exploration and chart-making took place, some measures had been taken to improve navigation downstream from Quebec City. As early as 1635 the Jesuit College in Quebec City taught courses in hydrography for Canadian pilots. This course was originally given by lay teachers but was soon taught by Jesuits known as Regius Professors of Hydrography. It became so widely acclaimed that in 1717 the Council of Marine in France granted the Jesuits the authority to issue pilot certificates.[5] A few years later, in 1729, the port captain of Quebec, La Richardière, was entrusted with the practical portion of the course, taking student pilots on board the vessel he was piloting.[6]

Aids to Navigation

A number of aids to navigation completed the set of measures intended to make sailing the waters of the St. Lawrence safer. In 1737 La Richardière ordered the construction of a truly ingenious range (a means of alignment) to make it easier for vessels to transit the Traverse – also known as the "Upper Traverse" – another particularly hazardous section on the river because of the proximity of many rocks, sandbanks and islets.[7]

---

[4]   Gilles Proulx, *Between France and New France* (Toronto: Dundurn Press, 1984), 78.

[5]   Canada, Royal Commission on Pilotage, *Study of Canadian Pilotage, Gulf and River St. Lawrence* (Ottawa: Queen's Printer, 1968–), vol. 4 (1970), 23.

[6]   Ibid., 24.

[7]   This "traverse" is located in the vicinity of Cap Tourmente, near Île d'Orléans. To this day, this passage remains extremely hazardous.

Unlike present-day ranges, which are made up of two lights that must be lined up in order to achieve the correct direction, La Richardière's appeared as a clearing 1,000 feet long and 100 feet wide on the Île aux Ruaux.

In a letter to the naval minister on October 1, 1737, the governor of New France, Beauharnois, and his intendant, Hocquart, identified the location of two other landmarks that were very likely built on the Île d'Orléans around 1739:

> There are still two marks to be set along Île d'Orléans. The first at the Rivière Delphine and the other at Pointe St-Jean. These two headlands being difficult to discern except under favourable weather conditions, being exceedingly low, the passage of the King's vessels and merchant vessels is often delayed.[8]

La Richardière, aware of the importance of these markers, suggested that actual stone walls be built on each of these two points of land. They were to be 30 feet wide and 25 to 80 feet high and 3 feet thick. Unfortunately, it is impossible to verify if these two structures were constructed to La Richardière's specifications. However, a document dated October 22, 1759, does confirm their existence and testifies to the continued interest in these aids to navigation until the end of the French regime:

> Every year, before the arrival of the King's vessels, the towers that had been expressly built on the Île d'Orléans had to be whitewashed and the trees that had grown up in the swath on Île au Ruaux cut down, to assist the ships' passage. The same precautions were taken for a 30-gun frigate as for a 60-gun frigate.[9]

These towers were neither more nor less than a range working on the same principle as the leading lights at Pointe Noire (at the mouth of the Saguenay) built two centuries later. "These two slightly open sections of wall will be the marks to follow in order to avoid the shoals."[10]

These, then, were the measures taken under French rule to assist navigation on the St. Lawrence River and in the Gulf. At first glance, it may seem surprising that the historiography reveals so few aids to navigation over such a long period of time; however, economic and military

---

[8]   Beauharnois and Hocquart to the naval minister, October 1, 1737, in Pierre-Georges Roy, *Le vieux Québec* (Lévis: n.p., 1931), vol. 2, 157 (translation).

[9]   France, Archives nationales, Colonie, C¹¹A, vol. 104, fol. 03-04, Vaudreuil et Bigot au ministre, Quebec, October 22, 1759 (translation).

[10] Pierre-Georges Roy, *Le vieux Québec,* 157 (translation).

considerations fully justified these small numbers. On the one hand, the sparse population of New France did not warrant the significant costs involved in building and maintaining a more extensive network of aids to navigation. On the other, fear of an English invasion had for many years curtailed any expansion of the system. "The primary objection to all these marks is that in rendering navigation both easy and secure for French vessels, our enemies would also benefit from them if they wished to advance against the colony."[11]

UNDER ENGLISH RULE

Immediately after the Conquest, the new British administrators were faced with the same shipping difficulties as their predecessors. Given the limited number of aids to navigation, the English were anxious to draw up a truly accurate chart of the river.

Charting the River

The task of charting the St. Lawrence was assigned to James Cook, known as the father of modern hydrography.[12] In the summer of 1760, Cook undertook the first series of surveys between Matane and the mouth of the Richelieu. The following year, he continued this work and produced a relatively accurate chart of this section of the river.[13] In 1762 and 1763, Cook surveyed the coastlines of Newfoundland, Labrador and the islands of Saint-Pierre and Miquelon.

Cook's work was carried on in the nineteenth century by someone who was just as much a celebrity in the world of hydrography: Admiral Henry Wolsey Bayfield of the Royal Navy in Canada. Between 1827 and 1841, Bayfield conducted a complete survey of the river from the western shores of Newfoundland right up to Montreal.[14]

Regulation Pilotage

Regulating pilotage services was also of primary importance to the new British administrators. In 1762 and 1768 two Governor's Ordinances created two pilot stations – one at Bic and the other at Île aux Coudres. These stations made approximately twenty pilots available to ships' masters who were unfamiliar with the St. Lawrence. Furthermore, and probably as an added incentive,

---

[11]   Ibid., 158 (translation).
[12]   Stanley Fillmore, *The Chartmakers: The History of Nautical Surveying in Canada* (Toronto: N.C. Press, 1983), 17.
[13]   Ibid., 20–21.
[14]   Ibid., 39.

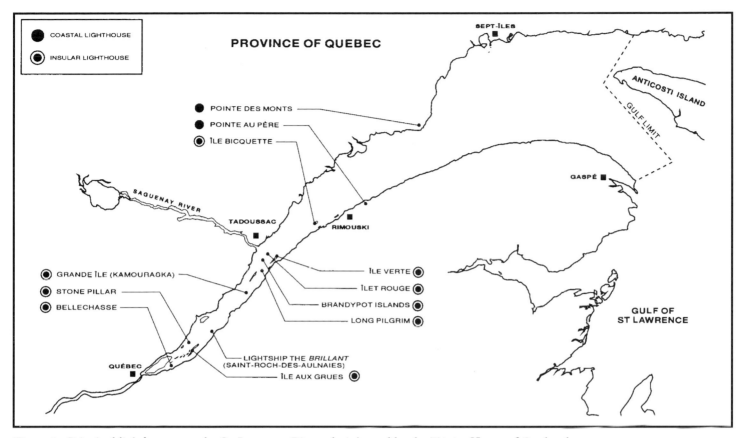

Figure 1. **Principal lighthouses on the St. Lawrence River administered by the Trinity House of Quebec between 1809 and 1862.**
(D. Boulet, Canadian Coast Guard, 1994)

these orders imposed pilotage dues that masters were obliged to pay even if they did not use the services of a pilot.[15]

Building Lighthouses

Despite all the efforts expended in exploration, cartography and pilotage, the number of marine disasters remained very high. Between June 3, 1776, and October 31, 1783, some sixty vessels were wrecked in the waters of the St. Lawrence.[16] Statistics such as these highlighted the pressing

---

[15]   Canada, Royal Commission on Pilotage, *Study of Canadian Pilotage,* vol. 4, 26.
[16]   National Archives of Canada (NAC), MG 21, Haldimand Papers, vol. 21885, 318.

need for a more highly developed network of aids to navigation. However, the new government was still unable to afford such a luxury. Therefore, only one lighthouse was built in the first fifty years of British rule, the lighthouse on Île Verte in the St. Lawrence River in 1809. This would, in fact, remain the river's only lighthouse until 1830. After this date, the number of lighthouses would grow slowly, but steadily, until Confederation in 1867. A total of seventeen lighthouses and one lightship were installed below Quebec City and in the Gulf of St. Lawrence between 1809 and 1862 (Appendix A and *Figures 1* and *2*). As will be seen in the following chapter, despite these lights, sailing from Newfoundland to Quebec would continue to be a perilous undertaking.

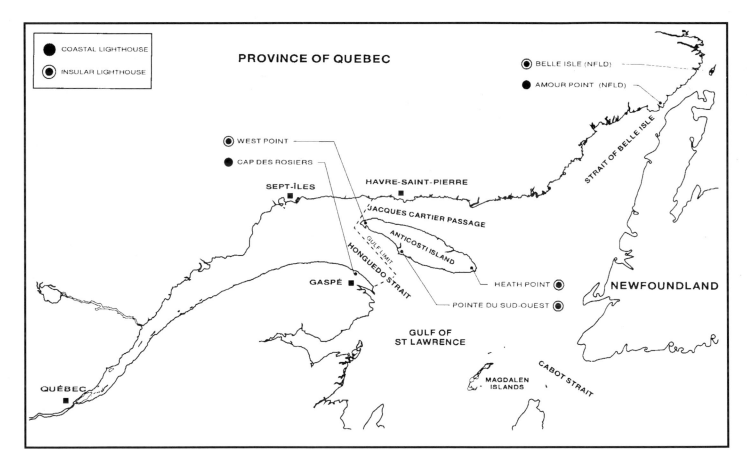

Figure 2. **Principal lighthouses in the Gulf of St. Lawrence administered by the Trinity House of Quebec between 1809 and 1862.**
(D. Boulet, Canadian Coast Guard, 1994)

Chapter Two

PERILOUS NAVIGATION IN THE NINETEENTH CENTURY

THE NAVIGABLE WATERWAY AND ITS PRIMARY OBSTACLES

The Strait of Belle Isle to the north of Newfoundland and Cabot Strait to the south were the two main access routes to the Gulf of St. Lawrence in the nineteenth century.

The Strait of Belle Isle

The shortest route to Quebec City for vessels originating in the British Isles was the Strait of Belle Isle, as Quebec City is located on the same latitude as London.[1] However, in spite of its geographical advantage, this strait was used very infrequently until the beginning of the twentieth century because of the almost continuous presence of icebergs and the many other difficulties inherent in the manoeuvring of sailing vessels. In any event, Admiral Bayfield's descriptions would be enough to discourage the most intrepid mariner:

> The soundings in the strait are so irregular that they afford very little assistance to a vessel at night or during the fogs which so frequently prevail … It is often at the temperature of the freezing point; bringing many icebergs into the strait, and frequently carrying them through it many miles up the Gulf. Some of these bergs ground in deep water, whilst others are continually changing their position. They are much more numerous in some seasons than in others, as I have seen 200 bergs and large pieces of ice in the strait in the month of August in one year, whilst there were not above half-a-dozen to be seen in the same month of the following season.[2]

Under these conditions, only a very few steamships carrying mail to and from the British Isles dared venture into the inhospitable waters of the Strait of Belle Isle in the mid-1800s. The

---

[1] J.-C. Lasserre, *Le Saint-Laurent, grande porte de l'Amérique* (Montreal: Hurtubise HMH, 1980), 31.
[2] Henry Wolsey Bayfield et al., *Sailing Directions for the Island of Newfoundland, and the Adjacent Coast of Labrador* (London: J. Imray & Sons, 1862), 75 (translation).

construction of three lighthouses at Belle Isle in 1858, 1880 and 1905 helped to increase the use of this passage in the early years of the twentieth century.

Cabot Strait

Entering the Gulf of St. Lawrence via Cabot Strait – the most frequently used route – was not without its own share of dangers. At the entrance of the strait, around St. Paul Island off the coast of Cape Breton, sailors had to use extreme caution, as emphasized by Robert Young, super-intendent of pilots, in 1831:

> Saint Paul Island … has been the cause of many shipwrecks, and given the nature of its shores, these tragedies have often been accompanied by a great loss of life. Completely encircled by steep cliffs, which are almost all inaccessible, there are few safe havens in bad weather, and the water generally being deep right up to the shore, vessels may be run up against these steep rocks without ever having touched bottom and be smashed into pieces in an instant.[3]

Barely three years later, the *Sibylle*, en route to Quebec City from Cromarty, Scotland, was shattered against the cliffs of St. Paul Island with the loss of all 316 immigrants on board.[4] In spite of this shipwreck and the many others that preceded it, it was not until 1839 that both ends of this island were equipped with lighthouses.

Once vessels had successfully made it past the dangers of St. Paul Island, other hazards littered the main shipping route to Quebec City. Île Brion and Bird Rocks, near the Magdalen Islands, caused at least seventeen wrecks between 1845 and 1857.[5] According to Captain Dutton of the Allan Line steamship company, a powerful current in this section often caused vessels to go off course and be driven directly onto Bird Rocks.[6] The seas around Île Brion also concealed myriad dangers:

[3]   Lower Canada, *Journals of the House of Assembly of Lower Canada*, vol. 40 (1831): "Rapport descriptif de l'Île Saint-Paul," quoted in Jean Leclerc, *Le Saint-Laurent et ses pilotes: 1805–1860* (Montreal: Leméac, 1991), 88 (translation).

[4]   Edward F. Bush, "The Canadian Lighthouse," in *Canadian Historic Sites: Occasional Papers in Archaeology and History*, no. 9 (1980), 40.

[5]   NAC, RG 11, B1 (a), vol. 230, subjet 227, February 28, 1860: John Page, "Report relative to the erection of Light Houses on the River & Gulf of St. Lawrence & Straits of Belle Isle."

[6]   Ibid., September 20, 1869.

Bryon Island … is rather more than 4 miles long … There are three reefs off Bryon Island. One off its east end extends near three-quarters of a mile to the north-eastward; another off the west end extends $1^1/2$ miles to the westward, and the third, off the sandy S.W. point, $1^1/3$ miles to the southward. The soundings extend … far off Bryon Island to seaward in every direction … but very great caution is requisite in approaching the reefs, for they are very steep, especially that which extends to the southward.[7]

Honguedo Passage

Advancing farther into the Gulf of St. Lawrence, mariners had to be particularly cautious in the Honguedo Passage, that wide corridor separating the Gaspé coastline from Anticosti Island. Despite the fact that there were three lighthouses on its southern shore by 1858, Anticosti continued to strike terror into the hearts of mariners at the end of the nineteenth century. The chief administrator of the Department of Marine and Fisheries in Quebec City, J.U. Gregory, reveals the primary reasons behind this fear:

> There are only three bays or harbours along the entire Anticosti coastline … These harbours are safe only for vessels of shallow draught, and only when the wind blows from a certain direction. Its shoals, which would be better named breakwaters, stretch one to two miles from the shore. Nowhere is it possible to find a haven or anchorage. Frequent fog, dangerous currents, and the absence of harbours have made this island the terror of seamen, and shipwrecks have often occurred under the most incomprehensible of circumstances.[8]

Gaspé Coast

As for the coastline of the Gaspé Peninsula, Admiral Bayfield simply advised that no one should attempt to approach it during cloudy or foggy nights, adding: "The shore along its whole extent, excepting in some of the bays, is of highly inclined slate and greywacke rocks, which would cut through a vessel's bottom in a very short time; and such is the impracticable nature of the country, that those who might escape to shore would run great risk of perishing from want before

---

[7] Henry Wolsey Bayfield et al., *Sailing Directions for the Gulf and River of St. Lawrence* (London: Hydrographic Office, 1843), vol. 1, 46–47.

[8] J.U. Gregory, *En racontant - Récits de voyages* … (Quebec: Darveau, 1886), 160 (translation).

they could reach a settlement."[9] In addition to the physical hazards described above, the climatic conditions were of great concern when sailing the waters of the Gulf of St. Lawrence:

> Among the difficulties of the navigation may be mentioned the ice. In spring the entrance and eastern parts of the Gulf are frequently covered with it, and vessels are sometimes beset for many days … In the fall of the year accidents from ice seldom occur, except when the winter commences suddenly, or when vessels linger imprudently late from the temptation of obtaining high freights. But all danger from ice is far less than that which arises from the prevalence of fogs: they may occur at any time during the open or navigable season, but are most frequent in the early part of summer … In the months of October and November the fogs and rain, that accompany easterly gales, are replaced by thick snow, which causes equal embarrassment to the navigator.[10]

Thus concludes this overview of the main obstacles confronting mariners in the waters of the Gulf of St. Lawrence. Having successfully sailed through Honguedo Passage, vessels finally entered the waters of the river itself.

Sailing up the River

Sailors' troubles were far from over, however. Sailing up the river to Quebec City was the most difficult part of their voyage. At a convention held in Rome in 1964, the president of the Canadian Board of Marine Underwriters stated: "The waters of northwestern Europe are the most dangerous in the world … followed by the northeastern section of North America, including the St. Lawrence River below Montreal."[11] If navigating the river could inspire this sort of declaration in 1964, one can easily imagine just how difficult it must have been a century earlier. In 1862 the Trinity House of Quebec had a mere eleven lighthouses to mark a route of over 200 miles between Pointe des Monts and Quebec City *(Figure 1)*. Along this same route, some eighty-four islands and islets obstruct the channel to a fairly significant degree.[12] Faced with this shortage of lighthouses, masters of foreign vessels took on board Canadian pilots from the official pilotage station established at Bic, then from 1905 onward, at Pointe au Père. Despite the

[9]   Henry Wolsey Bayfield et al., *Sailing Directions for the Gulf and River of St. Lawrence,* 89 (translation).

[10] Ibid., 4–5 (translation).

[11] Canada, Royal Commission on Pilotage, *Study of Canadian Pilotage, Gulf and River St. Lawrence* (Ottawa: Queen's Printer, 1968–), vol. 4 (1970), 83 (translation).

[12] Cécile Ouellet and Yvan Chouinard, *Autour des îles du Saint-Laurent* (Quebec: Ministère des Affaires culturelles, 1984), 15–22.

pilots' experience, however, fog could easily conceal an island, reef or sandbank, and running aground was always a possibility. Between Tadoussac and Pointe des Monts lay the mouth of the Saguenay, which was the most dangerous section, and it remains so to this day:

> The shoals, reefs and sandbanks are not the only hazards in this busy sector. The winds and currents are quite unusual, and so are the visibility conditions. The section where the Saguenay runs into the Gulf of St. Lawrence is very often shrouded in fog, especially during mornings in the month of August.[13]

Another hazard that had to be surmounted by pilots before reaching Quebec City was the infamous Lower Traverse, located the Île aux Coudres and L'Islet. Bayfield advised pilots to devote their full attention to this section, as it was recognized as being the most complicated on the entire St. Lawrence River. Even the most frequently used of the three channels available to pilots off Île aux Coudres presented significant challenges:

> Beyond Rivière du Sud [Montmagny] is a channel named the Traverse, which deserves mention from its importance as the main ship-channel, and the circumstance of its being remarkably narrow, although the river is here thirteen miles across; the Isle aux Coudres, the shoal of St. Rock, and another called the English Bank, contract the fair way to not more than 1320 yards (Captain Bayfield, R.N.) between the two buoys that mark the edge of the shoals; it is the most intricate part of the river below Quebec; the currents are numerous, irregular, and very strong, on which account large ships must consult the proper time of the tide to pass it without accident.[14]

SHIPWRECKS AND PROVISION DEPOTS

As we have just seen, navigating the waters of the St. Lawrence River and Gulf during the nineteenth century was always dangerous. Despite their usefulness, Bayfield's hydrographic surveys, the first network of lighthouses, and the pilotage service were not sufficient to reduce the number of shipwrecks in these waters.

---

[13] Jean Paradis, "Historique de la station de feux d'alignement de Pointe-Noire, P.Q.," internal report, Canadian Coast Guard, Laurentian Region, n.d.

[14] Joseph Bouchette, *The British Dominions in North America ...* (London: Longman, Orme, Brown, Green and Longman, 1832), 166.

The Toll

Because available data are only fragmentary, it is still impossible to know exactly how many shipwrecks occurred throughout the nineteenth century. However, a list drawn up by Henry Jessup, a Customs House collector, enables us to see the extent of the problem for the period spanning 1840 to 1849 (see Appendix B). Jessup reports a total of 233 accidents: an average of 17.5 per year, except for 1845 and 1847, when there were 46 and 47 accidents respectively.

In his study of pilotage on the St. Lawrence, Jean Leclerc points out that the 233 groundings and wrecks during this decade amounted to a loss of 1.8 percent of the 12,561 vessels used in trade with Quebec City in the same period.[15] As for the location of these groundings and shipwrecks, it would appear that the river was responsible for most of them: "The most disastrous year was 1846, when out of 1,467 merchant vessels, 47 were lost, 33 of them within the river's limits, between Saint-Anne-des-Monts and Portneuf."[16]

Another official list, entitled "Number of Lost, Wrecked, Stranded and Damaged Vessels, voyaging to and from the Port of Quebec, for the Years 1856 to 1866 Inclusive,"[17] records the loss of 674 vessels – almost triple the number of losses recorded for the period 1840–49. Using these numbers is somewhat problematic because the list does not specify the place where these marine casualties occurred. Nevertheless, regardless of the location, these accidents represented considerable losses for shipping companies in terms of both money and human life. The result was significant increases in marine insurance premiums. If Canada was going to compete with the Americans' Erie Canal, it would have to do everything necessary to decrease the number of shipwrecks taking place within its waters and thereby bring about a reduction in marine insurance premiums.

The Three Culprits

One of the leading politicians of his day – Deputy of Rimouski County Joseph-Charles Taché – when asked for his opinion on the matter of shipwrecks, said that he saw three main culprits: first, negligence on the part of ships' captains; second, a shortage of lighthouses along the coast; and third, lack of organization in the pilotage profession. In support of his first point, Taché noted that "there is not one wreck of our smaller coastal vessels for every five ocean-going vessels, although these larger ships are better able to withstand storms and are better equipped for navigation, and despite the fact that our coastal vessels travel in and out of the port of Quebec in

[15]   Jean Leclerc, *Le Saint-Laurent et ses pilotes,* 93.
[16]   Ibid. (translation).
[17]   Canada, Department of Transport, *GRCPW 1867*. See Appendix B, p. 97.

greater number than do the larger vessels."[18] Negligence on the part of ships' masters was also singled out for criticism by Bayfield as the main cause of shipwrecks within the limits of the St. Lawrence River.

> One might mention the practice of encumbering the decks of vessels with heavy loads that render them impossible to manoeuvre in foul weather or in the event of mishap, and perfectly incapable of steering clear of a lee-shore in heavy weather. Another cause is the detaining of vessels until the season is so far advanced that its crew (ill-clothed and weakened by excesses committed in Quebec City) is incapable of withstanding the blizzards and intense cold that are ordinarily encountered in the voyage near the mouth of the river and the gulf and which at times turn a vessel into a mass of ice.[19]

Setting Up Provision Depots

Rather than building a large number of lighthouses, the government of Lower Canada established several provision depots that would be of assistance to shipwrecked mariners. Some of these depots were the responsibility of a lightkeeper, while others were kept by local residents. By 1836, seven depots had been set up along the river below Quebec City.[20] Two of these – which were not connected with a lighthouse – were located on the South Shore at Cap-Chat and at Rivière-la-Madeleine. On the North Shore, a single depot at Pointe des Monts was intended to serve the entire St. Lawrence estuary. The remaining four were located on Anticosti Island at South Point, Southwest Point, East Point and at Ellis Bay, at the western end of the island. The forty-seven shipwrecks recorded on this island between 1828 and 1860[21] amply justified the placement of these four depots. Furthermore, when it came to locating the provisions, nothing was left to chance:

> And when an unfortunate vessel wrecks upon these shores, and the men of her crew, half-drowned and often only half-clothed, reach the shore, they have only to follow the bank in any direction and they will soon see boards nailed to trees that will surely guide them.

[18] *Revue d'histoire du Bas-Saint-Laurent,* "Le rapport Taché," vol. 6, no. 1 (January–April 1979), 31.

[19] "Correspondence between Captain Bayfield and the Honourable W.H. Hewitt (October 4, 1850)," quoted in Jean Leclerc, *Le St. Laurent et ses pilotes,* 93 (translation).

[20] Jean Leclerc, *St. Laurent et ses pilotes,* 93–94.

[21] Narcisse Rosa, *La construction des navires à Québec et ses environs: grèves et naufrages* (Quebec: L. Brousseau, 1897), 195–97.

In many directions one sees boards painted with hands, fingers pointing in the direction to follow, and indicating along the way the distance to the first provision depot, or the first house of refuge.[22]

Keeping the Depots

Keepers of the depots were subject to very strict regulations regarding the distribution of their supplies. Crew members were required to have consumed all provisions recovered from the wreck before being permitted to break open the stores. A daily ration set at three-quarters of a pound of pork, a pound of flour and half a pound of peas could then be distributed to each of the shipwrecked sailors[23] until they were able to make their way back to Quebec City. Each ration was carefully weighed by the depot keeper, who was required to maintain a detailed inventory of the foodstuffs distributed for each shipwreck. These statistics were extremely important for the administrators of Trinity House, because they could then claim repayment from ship captains for the expenses run up by survivors throughout their stay at the provision depot. Keeping these inventories also allowed Trinity House to maintain strict control over all of the foodstuffs at the various depots – just in case some depot keepers were tempted to put a few extra pieces of bacon on their own tables.

For the lightkeepers at Pointe des Monts, Southwest Point (Anticosti) and Heath Point (East Point, Anticosti), administering a provision depot was only one of the many aspects of the job.

---

[22]   J.U. Gregory, *En racontant*, 103–4.
[23]   APQ-FMTQ, 1, A, Minutes, vol. 6, October 18, 1839.

Chapter Three

AN ANONYMOUS LABOUR

A PROFILE OF THE LIGHTKEEPERS

Charles Hambelton

Charles Hambelton, an English-speaker of Scottish origin, was the first lightkeeper on the St. Lawrence. His appointment to Île Verte (then Green Island) in 1809 began a long tradition of lightkeeping that would last for 179 years – until 1988.[1] Hambelton was related through marriage to the Rollets, who had distinguished themselves during the American War of Independence, and to Samuel Holland, mariner and hydrographer.[2] As a sea captain himself, Hambelton was able to emphasize his knowledge of the river and Gulf of St. Lawrence in support of his application for lightkeeper[3] *(Figures 3 and 4)*. Another point in his favour, and one which in all probability reassured the administrators of Trinity House in Quebec City, was that

Figure 3.
Île Verte Lighthouse, east of Rivière-du-Loup, in the first half of the twentieth century.
(*Canadian Coast Guard Archives*)

[1]   APQ-FMTQ, 2, III, Aids to Navigation, A, 12.3, Île Verte, April 11, 1807, and October 28, 1811.
[2]   Comité des Loisirs de l'île, *Ile Verte avant-hier, au phare ...* (L'Isle-Verte-en-île: Lévesque-Langlois, 1990), 11.
[3]   APQ-FMTQ, 2, III, Aids to Navigation, A, 12.3, Île Verte, April 15, 1807.

Hambelton claimed to be aware of the dangers posed by an ill-tended lighthouse. When accompanied with assurances like these, such an application was very likely to be accepted, particularly as Charles Hambelton had applied for the position in 1807, two years before the official opening of the lighthouse, and as his application was supported by about twenty people, one of whom was John Richardson, inspector general of lighthouses for Trinity House.[4]

Did Hambelton's eagerness discourage other applicants? This may indeed be so, as no other application appears in the Trinity House archives. In any event, Hambelton's experience, coupled with the prominence of his relatives, earned him the position and at the same time set a

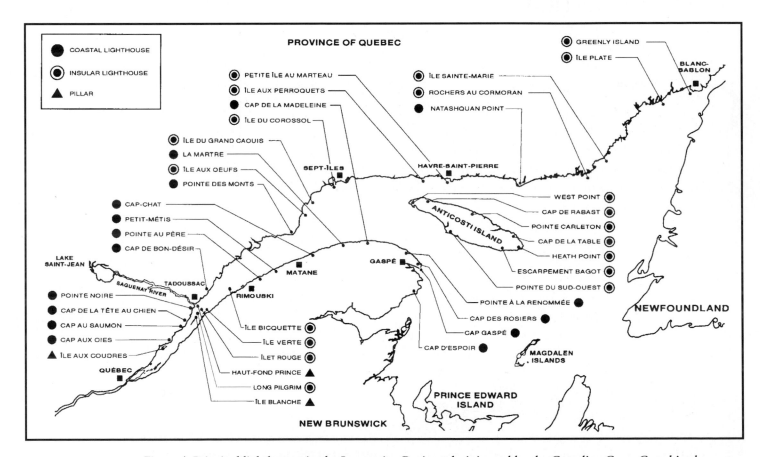

Figure 4. **Principal lighthouses in the Laurentian Region administered by the Canadian Coast Guard in the 1980s.**
(D. Boulet, Canadian Coast Guard, 1994)

---

4   Ibid., April 11 and 30, 1807.

precedent for lightkeeping appointments, which would remain highly political for more than a century and half.

Patronage

Under the administration of Trinity House, an application for the position of lightkeeper had first to be submitted by this organization to the provincial secretary; the official nomination ratified by the governor general would then follow.[5] Therefore, once an application had been approved at the Trinity House level, it was then subject to the whims of the political regime.

This practice continued under the administration of the Department of Marine and Fisheries.

> Before recommending a person to His Excellency in Council for the position of light-keeper, the Minister of Marine usually consults the member of Parliament for the county or district in which the vacancy has occurred (if he is a supporter of the Government), and obtains his recommendation of a suitable person for the appointment. There is no system of promotion among the keepers, and it is understood that the appointments are usually made through political influence.[6]

While the procedure became less blatant over time, political appointments were still taking place well into the second half of the twentieth century. A significant number of the last lightkeepers in Quebec admitted that political influence had played an important role in the appointment of their grandfathers, their fathers and sometimes even of themselves.

Background

In spite of the political meddling that often worked more against them than for them, applicants for the position of lightkeeper first had to meet certain criteria before they could hope to have their applications considered. Here too it is interesting to observe the conservatism of the profession of lightkeeping throughout its existence in Quebec: not one of the administrations responsible for lightkeeping required that applicants have any specialized training. Only a few years before lightkeeping disappeared in 1988, the average schooling of lightkeepers in the Laurentian Region (administrative region for Quebec) was Grade 7.[7] And yet, is that so surprising? "You

---

[5]   APQ-FMTQ, 1, A, Minutes, vol. 9, November 27, 1849, 25.

[6]   William Smith, "The Lighthouse System of Canada," a paper … read … 1st Sept. 1884, 19.

[7]   Interview with Lise Cloutier, superintendent of lights for the Laurentian Region, September 25, 1987.

can't learn about the sea from books. It is tasted in childhood on sea-sprayed lips, it is told during evenings around the family table, it is smelt in the oilskins worn by fathers coming through the door; to live off the sea, one must live with the sea."[8] However, not everyone who wanted to become a lightkeeper was successful; despite the seemingly simple criteria for admission described below, lightkeeping has always been restricted to a very select group.

Requirements

The prospective lightkeeper had to fulfil few requirements. In 1869, he was required to be between 18 and 50 years old, to be in good health, and to have good eyesight. Colour-blind applicants were rejected immediately, as some of the light stations used semaphore, a communication system based on the use of flags of various shapes and colours (see "Signal Service" on page 50). The applicant also had to be of good character, be able to read and write, and have a knowledge of at least the basic rudiments of arithmetic. Various certificates were required to confirm that the applicant had met these prerequisites. Finally, the applicant was required to provide a letter of recommendation from his previous employer describing both the position he had held and his character (Appendix C).

At first glance, it would appear that hundreds of applicants could have satisfied these requirements, and many applications were in fact sent to the various administrations responsible for lighthouse management from 1809 onward.

The Applicants

It is interesting to ponder the diversity of people interested in such a solitary post. Farmer, fisherman, merchant, innkeeper, mason, captain in the militia, teacher and, surprisingly, even a French count and lawyer – all at some point sent in their application for the position. However, Trinity House was most interested in men recruited from among the ranks of pilots, navigators, ship captains or ordinary seamen. The reason for this preference for applicants who had already worked in one of the seagoing trades is obvious. As Charles Hambelton noted in his application, no one is more aware of the dangers of an ill-tended lighthouse than a mariner.

From Father to Son

Another interesting aspect of lightkeeping is the handing down of positions from father to son. While this custom is most evident in the latter decades, it is nevertheless rooted in an earlier era.

---

[8]   Jean-Paul Dumoutier and René Gast, *Des phares et des hommes* (Paris: Éd. Maritimes J.-C. Lallès, 1985), 64 (translation).

The lighthouse at Île Verte is an excellent example. For more than 137 years, this lighthouse was in the capable hands of the Lindsays,[9] a family of Scottish origin that held the position between 1827 and 1964. The North Shore of the St. Lawrence has a similar record of continuity with the light at Pointe des Monts, tended by the Fafard family for more than 81 years.[10]

Admittedly, these two cases are exceptional; nevertheless, a number of archival documents reveal that lightkeeping positions were handed down through generations throughout the nineteenth and twentieth centuries. These "inheritances" did require approval by the administration, however, as all applicants had to meet the same basic requirements. Only months before the last lightkeepers left their posts in Quebec, the superintendent of lights for the Laurentian Region stated in an interview that

> the lightkeepers we have right now are in positions that have been handed down from father to son, or brother or cousin. There is always a blatant family connection. This is their life right from day one; for them, living at a light station is part of their world.[11]

A Man's Job

Also characteristic of the position of lightkeeper throughout its history in Quebec is that it would always remain a strictly male endeavour. Unlike our American neighbour, where more than thirty widows had taken over their husbands' positions as official lightkeeper by 1851,[12] no woman would ever succeed in securing this position in Quebec.

The first woman to apply for the position was Charlotte Angélique Rollet Hambelton, widow of Charles Hambelton, first lightkeeper in Quebec. In her application submitted April 21, 1827,[13] Mrs. Hambelton contended that for more than eighteen years the light at Île Verte was for the most part under her control and guardianship, and that since the death of her husband earlier that year, she had been fulfilling the duties of keeper in accordance with the rules and procedures laid down by Trinity House. She therefore requested that the position be granted to her personally or to her son, Thomas, stressing that her husband had left her no means of support. Her petition did not kindle any sympathy in the hearts of administrators at Trinity House. Robert Noël Lindsay, apprentice pilot and seaman from Quebec City, became the second Île Verte lightkeeper. At least three other requests of this sort were received by Trinity House prior to

[9]   Comité des Loisirs de l'Île, *Ile Verte avant-hier*, 11–12.

[10]   Pierre Frenette, *Le phare historique de Pointe-des-Monts et ses gardiens* (Baie-Comeau: Société historique de la Côte-Nord, 1990), 3.

[11]   Interview with Lise Cloutier, September 25, 1987 (translation).

[12]   Elinor De Wire, "Women of the Lights," *American History Illustrated*, vol. 21, no. 10 (1987), 43.

[13]   APQ-FMTQ, 2, III, Aids to Navigation, A, 12.3, Île Verte, April 21, 1827.

1867, but each time these widows met with the same refusal from the administrators. One of these women, the widow of Zoël Bédàrd of the Pointe des Monts Light, was told that she could not be hired "because of her advanced age and because the position of lightkeeper must needs be filled by a man whose services are at all times more competent."[14]

The Reasons Behind the Choice

A profile of lightkeepers on the St. Lawrence would be incomplete without a look into why they chose this career. In the many cases where the position had been handed down within families, this question appears rather pointless – a love of the work naturally led these men to seek employment doing what they had already been doing from a very young age. But what about the applicants who had been employed in other areas? Why did some of them deliberately give up better-paying jobs to become lightkeepers? This last question was put to thirty former keepers from the Gaspé Peninsula, Lower St. Lawrence, Saguenay Region, North Shore and Anticosti Island. A significant number replied that they were looking for employment close to home, and it should be pointed out that all the keepers interviewed were originally from the area in which they worked. The lack of employment that has always been prevalent in these remote regions forced more than one of these men to leave for the cities or logging camps, or even to join the navy. After a few years of being away, a number of them felt the need to be closer to their families. The opening of a lightkeeping position in their area gave them that opportunity.

An Enviable Position

While never particularly well paid, the position of lightkeeper brought with it a material security that no other employment at that time could guarantee. This advantage did kindle some envy. These comments from the widow of the last of the famous Lindsay dynasty of Île Verte lightkeepers leave little doubt:

> There was jealousy and it made trouble for my husband. And there were some people who tried to make him lose his job, especially at election time, or, like … when there was smuggling. They said he had hidden what was known as "miquelon" – bootleg whiskey. He was supposed to have hidden a boatload of "miquelon," a load of the bootleg liquor that people used to sell in those days. And then the police came … It was real hard on him. And it was just jealousy. It was two people on the island who really wanted his job, and they made that report. But it was all lies.[15]

---

14   Pierre Frenette, *Le phare historique de Pointe-des-Monts*, 23 (translation).
15   Interview with Mrs. Freddy Lindsay, May 1, 1991 (translation).

Other keepers revealed that the slightest delay in lighting or, worse yet, the early extinguishing of their beacon was immediately reported to the administration, either by seamen or by conscientious local inhabitants.

Fortunately, the job was not all troubles and problems – quite the opposite. Lightkeepers also had their moments in the limelight: at one time they were among the few, if not the only, public servants in their small communities. As such they were among the dignitaries of the area, and the weighty responsibility of their position earned them widespread admiration and respect.

DAILY ROUTINE

In Quebec, lightkeeping changed drastically in the mid-1970s with the arrival of automation.[16] The first phase involved refurbishing a station's traditional equipment so that it would be fully automated and monitored remotely from various monitoring stations *(Figures 5 and 7 to 9)*. From then on, the keeper's job was merely to ensure that the new electronic equipment was functioning properly *(Figure 6)*, to inform the administration of any anomalies at the station, and to take care of general maintenance and domestic chores.

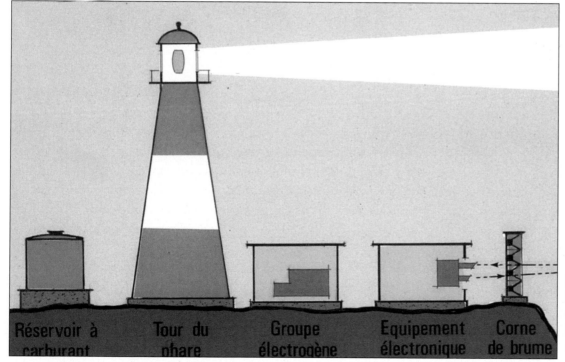

Réservoir à carburant   Tour du phare   Groupe électrogène   Equipement électronique   Corne de brume

Figure 5. **Drawing of a fully automated light station. Highly sophisticated electronic equipment now fills the role of lightkeeper.**
(Canadian Coast Guard)

---

[16] Interview with Lise Cloutier, September 25, 1987.

Figure 6.

When light stations were first automated, keepers were responsible for ensuring that the new electronic equipment was working reliably.
(Canadian Coast Guard Archives, no date)

Before automation, lightkeeping was directly related to the proper functioning of the various pieces of equipment constituting the aids to navigation. The keeper was therefore responsible for lighting and extinguishing the lighthouse lamp, ensuring that it did not smoke, cleaning and maintaining all the optical equipment, winding up the lamp's clockwork rotating mechanism, activating the fog signal, seeing to the general maintenance of the station buildings and doing any necessary mechanical upkeep. In addition, he had to provide for his own sustenance and that of his family.

This brief overview of daily chores is still an inadequate representation of the amount of work required of lightkeepers. To do them justice, I have attempted here to depict a typical day based on their correspondence and, more particularly, on the various editions of rules and regulations governing their activities. While ten rules were sufficient to cover their duties in 1809,[17]

---

[17]   APQ-FMTQ, 1, A, Minutes, vol. 1, September 19, 1809, 399–402; this first body of regulations was revised and expanded around 1858 (APQ-FMTQ, 1, B, Correspondence, vol. 4, *c.* 1858–67).

Figure 7. In the foreground, the electronic fog horn; behind, the small building to the left houses the visibility sensor and the one to the right the electric generator. This equipment can be found at all automated light stations.
(Photo: M. Plamondon, Canadian Coast Guard, no date)

Figure 8. In the foreground, the visibility sensor, and behind, the electronic fog horn. When the visibility becomes slightly too obscured, the sensor engages the electronic fog horn.
(Photo: M. Plamondon, Canadian Coast Guard, no date)

Figure 9.
Rivière-au-Renard monitoring station on the Gaspé Peninsula. The slightest anomaly at an
automated light station is immediately detected by a monitoring station.
(Photo: M. Plamondon, Canadian Coast Guard, no date)

Figure 10.
**Îlet Rouge Lighthouse across from the Saguenay, in the 1980s. When it began operating
in 1848, this light used twenty-four oil lamps and as many reflectors.**
(Photo: D. Chamard, Canadian Coast Guard)

Figure 11.
Lighthouse at Cap de la Tête au Chien (Charlevoix) in the 1980s. Maintenance of the stairway (325 steps) and numerous footbridges added to the keeper's painting duties.
(Photo: D. Chamard, Canadian Coast Guard)

Figure 12.
In foggy weather, light stations sounded a signal that would enable vessels to plot their position. Here the station on Île aux Perroquets in the Mingan Islands is surrounded by fog.
(Canadian Coast Guard Archives, no date)

Figure 13.
Cap des Rosiers Light on the Gaspé Peninsula in the 1980s. Keepers all dreamed of being
assigned to a coastal station near a village where they could buy anything they needed.
(Photo: D. Chamard, Canadian Coast Guard)

Figure 14.
Île Verte Light Station to the east of Rivière-du-Loup, February 1990.
(Canadian Coast Guard Archives)

Figure 15.
Île aux Perroquets Light in the Mingan Islands in the 1980s. On an insular station, keepers had to deal with a harsh life and restrictive work.
(Canadian Coast Guard Archives)

Figure 16.
Lower Traverse Pillar, off Île aux Coudres. Pillar lights were without doubt the harshest and most isolated of Quebec's light stations, particularly since keepers were unable to have their families live with them.
(Canadian Coast Guard Archives, no date)

Figure 17.
Île Blanche Pillar Light off Cacouna.
(Canadian Coast Guard Archives, no date)

the 1912 edition was a booklet of thirty-nine pages with no fewer than 193 rules and instructions.[18] This volume is one of the most important sources of information because it deals with the handling of some pieces of equipment that would remain in use for more than a century.

Mornings

All work preparatory to lighting the lamps had to be done in the morning, and this was no mean task, as the entire interior and exterior of the lantern had to be in perfect condition by evening. Some lighthouses, such as the one on Îlet Rouge, opposite the mouth of the Saguenay *(Figure 10),* could use more than twenty oil lamps (Appendix A) similar to those used by our forefathers as light sources. The effort required to maintain each of these lamps provides us with a fairly good idea of the magnitude of the task awaiting the keeper every morning.

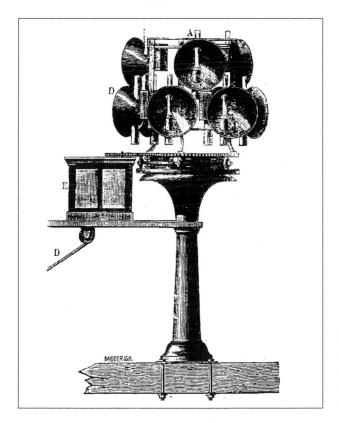

Figure 18.
Lighthouses that operated on the catoptric system could use more than twenty lamps and reflectors. Porpoise and wolffish oil were used to fuel them until 1863.
(Louis Figuier, "Les phares," in Les merveilles de la science *[Paris: Jouvet, 1867–70], vol. 4, 428)*

---

[18]   Canada, Department of Marine and Fisheries, *Rules and Instructions for the Guidance of Lightkeepers* (Ottawa: Government Printing Bureau, 1912), 1–39.

Trimming the Wicks

Immediately following the extinguishing of the lamps, the curtains were drawn over the windows of the lantern, and linen covers were placed over the lenses or reflectors. These precautions were taken to protect the lenses from the sun's rays, which tarnished the reflectors and prisms.

The keeper then hastened to trim the lamps' wicks, these being easier to trim while still slightly warm. The keeper had to be meticulous in this task, as a poorly trimmed wick caused soot to build up on the lamp glass and even on the reflector. A layer of soot greatly reduced the light's efficiency – not to mention the drudgery of cleaning that would follow.

Cleaning the Reflectors and Lenses

If, by good fortune, the lamps had not smoked too much during the night, the keeper got off with merely having to wipe the reflectors. If he was not so lucky, each of the reflectors (one per lamp) had to be dismantled and transported to the service room beneath the lantern for a complete polishing *(Figure 18)*. This task took hours: reflectors could be 18 to 22 inches in diameter and 7 to 18 inches deep,[19] and each one had to be cleaned with a mixture of iron oxide rouge and sweet oil. They were then polished with dry rouge and a clean chamois. Whether the wicks smoked or not, this job had to be done at least twice a week; the keeper had no way of getting out of it because a regulation stipulated that "any scratches in the silvering must be due to dust or careless work, and the keeper will be held accountable for them."[20]

As for the dioptric or refractory lights *(Figure 19)*, they too required their fair share of cleaning drudgery. In fact, the hundreds of glass prisms and the optic's lenses also had to be cleaned daily. They were dusted with a moistened linen duster, then patiently dried all over with a chamois.

Apparatus and Oil

Maintaining the lamp apparatus was also part of the morning chores. The keeper had to pay particular attention to reducing problems in the burning of the oil or kerosene during the night. All parts of the burners that came in contact with the flame therefore had to be cleaned and polished. The other parts had to be kept perfectly clean, particularly the ventilating holes. Once this job was completed, all the reservoirs had to be filled with oil that had been previously filtered to

---

[19]   According to George D. O'Farrell, Canada's inspector of lighthouses in 1900. "Notes on the lighthouses of the Province before the Literary and Historical Society of Quebec," *The Transactions of the Literary and Historical Society of Quebec*, no. 24, Session 1900–1902 (Québec: Le Soleil, 1902), 24–36.

[20]   Canada, Department of Marine and Fisheries, *Rules and Instructions*, Regulation No. 25, 6.

remove impurities. Sources reveal that right up until 1859 there were a number of complaints from the early keepers regarding the poor quality of the oil that was used.[21] There were also complaints about porpoise oil, which was so thick that it had to be heated in order to be liquefied. In cold weather, filling the reservoirs had to be put off until early evening so that the warmed oil would remain liquid until lamp-lighting time.

Lantern Panes

The morning progressed with the cleaning of the lantern panes. A seemingly simple task, it could at times become one of mammoth proportions, as described by Robert Noël Lindsay, second lightkeeper at Île Verte: "For some time now the insects swarm the lantern to such an extent that it can be likened to a curtain before the light."[22] The fact that Lindsay took the time to inform the administration of the problem reveals his utter dismay in dealing with this situation. Further, by taking this step, he covered himself in the event of complaints from seamen. Frost,

Figure 19.
Dioptric apparatus used at the Upper Traverse Pillar, to the northeast of the Île d'Orléans, from 1901 to 1931. The clockwork mechanism rotating the lens carriage is clearly visible.
(Canadian Coast Guard Archives, no date)

---

21   APQ-FMTQ, 2, III, Aids to Navigation, A, 1-25, 1806–70.
22   Ibid., 12.3, Île Verte, October 3, 1864 (translation).

like insects, could also obscure the light through the lantern panes, and in order to clear them, the keeper had sometimes to brave violent gales on the narrow gallery encircling the lantern.

The morning's chores ended with the winding up of the weights driving the lamp's rotating mechanism – weights that could tip the scales at several hundred pounds. Maurice Thibeault, the most experienced of the Quebec lightkeepers, still clearly remembers this task, which he repeated thousands upon thousands of times during his forty-three years on the lights. "At Bicquette, it took 810 turns and it took ten minutes to raise the weight. It was rough … there were three speeds on the crank, depending on the guy's strength."[23] Now that everything was ready for lighting the lamp in the evening, the keeper could take a few hours of well-deserved rest.

Afternoons

Lightkeepers had no fixed duties for the afternoon. However, they usually spent this time of day working on providing for their own subsistence or on the general upkeep of the various station buildings.

General Upkeep

Item 75 of the *Rules and Instructions for the Guidance of Lightkeepers* (1912) provides a splendid summary of the government's philosophy on the lightkeepers' maintenance duties:

> Keepers must not only keep their lanterns, lighthouses, dwelling houses and out-buildings clean and tidy and in good repair, but must also keep the surroundings of their stations in a state to reflect credit on the Government, and be a model to the neighbourhood. Fences must be kept in proper repair, and those in the immediate vicinity of the buildings, neatly painted or whitewashed. All firewood and chips must be confined to proper yards, and no Government tools, vehicles or supplies, must be left exposed to the weather.[24]

In other words, the entire station had to shine like a new pin, and an annual inspection ensured that these high standards of orderliness were maintained. Failure to adhere to any one of the station maintenance regulations was liable to be severely punished, and could even result in

---

[23]   Interview with Maurice Thibeault, April 30, 1991 (translation).

[24]   Canada, Department of Marine and Fisheries, *Rules and Instructions*, 15.

dismissal of the keeper. The apparent free hand accorded to lightkeepers was therefore entirely relative.

At some stations, painting could be a much bigger job than at others. The Cap de la Tête au Chien Light, for example, had a stairway of 325 steps and numerous footbridges, which added to the maintenance of the station buildings *(Figure 11)*. According to one of its last keepers, between forty and forty-five gallons of paint were used every year.[25]

Making Ends Meet

As for the livelihood of keepers and their families, it should be noted that only accommodation was provided. Consequently, as soon as they arrived at a posting, keepers were required to cut their own firewood and secure their own food and provisions. Because of their relatively low wages, most keepers kept a vegetable garden and some kept farm animals, which added to their chores. Hunting and fishing also helped put food on their tables. With all these activities, keepers had no trouble keeping busy in the afternoon.

Evenings

Tending the Light

Duties that were directly related to the light began again in the evening, one hour before sundown. If the morning's chores had been done properly, the keeper had only to remove the covers protecting the reflectors, open the curtains, and begin lighting the lamps so that they would be shining at full force by nightfall and would continue to do so until sunrise. But even after he had seen to all this, his work was not over. According to regulations issued in 1809, the first keepers were required to trim the wicks of the lamps every three hours, "taking particular care that they are exactly even on the top."[26] They also had to keep almost continuous watch over their lamps because the slightest impurity in the oil could cause wicks to flare and blacken the reflectors. This problem had to be avoided at all costs for safety reasons and also because it could mean hours of cleaning for the keeper. It was therefore in the keeper's interest to maintain a careful watch over his equipment.

The fuel and lamps obviously improved greatly over the years. However, keepers still had to remain vigilant during the interminable watches in case there was the slightest weakening of

25   Interview with Fortunat Savard, May 13, 1991.
26   APQ-FTMQ, 1, A, Minutes, vol. 1, September 19, 1809, 400 (translation).

the lamp's light. The more experienced of the keepers who were interviewed remembered the days of oil lamps and kerosene burners. Some of them had successfully rigged an alarm bell that would allow them to get a couple of hours of sleep during the night: when a lamp flared up, the flame would burn through a length of string attached to a weight which would in turn cut off the fuel flow and ring a bell in the keeper's room. With a smile, one of the keepers of the light at Cap d'Espoir on the Gaspé Peninsula confided, "The people in Quebec City eventually knew about it, but didn't say anything."[27]

Time Keeping

Another anecdote illustrates the inventiveness of the keepers. Since they were required to light their lamps one hour before sundown, it was important to know how to determine when that was. Roland Boudreau, keeper at the Île au Marteau Light, relates how his father, also a keeper, taught him how to tell when it was one hour before sunset: "It's when you stretch your arm out in front of your eyes and place your hand between the sun and the horizon: if there is just enough space for four fingers, it's time to light the lamp, because the width of each finger equals fifteen minutes."[28] When it was raining or foggy, lighting simply took place earlier and, from daybreak, the keeper's unrelenting daily routine carried on as usual.

Night Watches

The keeper's workday as described here might appear to be more than one man could handle, since rest periods were virtually nonexistent. Fortunately, keepers got help from their family members, and the first stations were soon manned with one or even two assistants to help the principal keeper. Watches were therefore established to ensure that the equipment was functioning properly during the night. However, only the principal keeper was entrusted with the responsibility of filling in the daily log for expenses and for the light station's operations. In this log the keeper scrupulously listed the times at which the lamp was lighted and extinguished, the weather conditions, workers' absences, and the various maintenance and painting jobs. Fog signal operations were written up in a second daily log. The keeper was required to send a copy of these two reports to the administration once a month.

---

[27]   Interview with Gordon Trachi, June 18, 1991: a similar mechanism appears to have been used at the lighthouse at Île aux Perroquets in the Mingan Islands.

[28]   Rodrigue Gignac, "Les phares du Saint-Laurent," Montreal, Maison de Radio-Canada; series of thirteen programs produced by CBV Québec, Transcript and Product Services, Program No. 8, 16 (translation).

FOG SIGNALS

Before the advent of such sophisticated aids to navigation as the radio beacon and radar, fog was considered to be one of the greatest dangers that mariners could face. At night, fog could render even the strongest of lights virtually useless, with its beam of light being almost completely dispersed or absorbed by water droplets. During the day, the situation was just as dangerous because it was impossible for mariners to follow the shoreline or any other landmark.

Fortunately, it had long been known that a sound signal could take over from a light and, in foggy conditions, enable vessels to determine their position with a certain amount of accuracy. A number of devices were therefore tested in the nineteenth century in order to increase the efficiency of fog signals as aids to navigation *(Figure 20)*.

Role Played by Pointe au Père

The light station at Pointe au Père on the Lower St. Lawrence played an important role in the testing of equipment at the turn of the century. In 1903 it was selected by the Department of Marine and Fisheries as a testing station for two new fog signals, the diaphone and the Scotch siren, before these were installed at other Canadian light stations.[29] Among the other fog signals

Figure 20.
Fog horn used at the Belle Isle Lighthouse in the Strait of Belle Isle, at the turn of the century.
(Canadian Coast Guard Archives, no date)

---

[29]   Canada, Parliament, Chamber of Commons, *Sessional Papers*, no. 21, 1903, "Annual Report of the Chief Engineer of the Department of Marine and Fisheries" (Ottawa: Queen's Printer, 1904), 46.

used at Quebec light stations since 1809 were the fog gun, steam whistle, guncotton cartridge and submarine bell. Fog signals currently in use at Canadian light stations date from the early 1970s. Visitors can learn about these various types of signals at the Parks Canada exhibit located in the fog horn building at the Pointe au Père station.

Watching for the Signs

Unlike the lighting of the lamp, activating the fog signal was not part of the keeper's daily duties. However, keepers were very aware of the fact that they could be required to start up and tend the fog signal at any time of the day or night, and keep on monitoring it for an indefinite period. As "objective" criteria, every station had a certain number of landmarks that could be used to determine visibility; if one or more of them disappeared from the horizon, it was time to activate the fog signal. Keepers therefore had to keep a constant lookout for these landmarks as soon as fog, rain or snow began to reduce visibility around the station.

Fog – The Intangible Foe

According to a statistical survey of all regions across Canada conducted by Environment Canada,[30] the estuary of the St. Lawrence is the area most affected by dense fog between the months of May and September, which is the busiest period in the shipping season *(Figure 12)*. According to this same study, the Southwest Point Light Station on Anticosti Island holds the Canadian fog record for this same period: 66.6 days.

Extra Work

These types of statistics give us some idea of the extra work that had to be done by lightkeepers at stations on Anticosti Island and the Gaspé Peninsula, given that these areas are renowned for their extremely dense fog.[31] Some keepers revealed that they had experienced several consecutive days of fog or sometimes entire weeks. According to Gordon Trachi, former keeper at several stations on Anticosti Island, this type of experience was among the most taxing, since someone had to be in the vicinity of the fog signal equipment day and night. The slightest anomaly in one of the signal's components had to be repaired immediately. Keepers became so used to the attendant noise that they set up cots right inside the fog signal building. This allowed them to catch a few minutes of sleep here and there. Ironically, keepers woke up with a start as soon as the

30   Jean-Claude Lasserre, *Le Saint-Laurent, grande porte de l'Amérique* (Montreal: Hurtubise HMH, 1980), 468–69.
31   Ibid.

engines or signal stopped working. The very first St. Lawrence lightkeepers had no such opportunity to sleep next to their equipment because at that time cannon shots were used as fog signals. This system was gradually replaced by the guncotton cartridge, a device that created loud explosions. Depending on the station's code, the blasts had to occur every fifteen minutes or even every five minutes. Keepers must have heaved huge sighs of relief when the fog finally lifted.

RELATED DUTIES

The various duties described above lay at the very heart of lightkeeping, since they were directly related to the basic equipment at each of the Laurentian Region's stations. However, a number of keepers had extra duties because other aids to navigation were in use or because of the strategic location of their stations.

Marine Surveillance

During the War of 1812 between Great Britain and the United States, the Île Verte Light Station was used as an observation post by the British Admiralty to spot incursions by the American fleet into this sector of the St. Lawrence River. In addition to his usual duties, the lightkeeper was required to watch out for signals sent by the schooner *St. Lawrence*, patrolling off the island. During the day, a red pennant hoisted on the foremast below a blue ensign signalled the arrival of an enemy fleet. When he received the signal, the keeper was to leave the lamp unlighted until new orders were received, and send a message overland to the governor general at Quebec City as soon as possible. At night or in fog, two closely timed cannon shots fired from the *St. Lawrence* followed five minutes later by another two shots signalled the presence of an enemy vessel in the area. The keeper was then to extinguish the light and send a message overland to the governor general.[32]

The military authorities once again sought out the services of lightkeepers during the Second World War, when in 1942 German submarines attacked and sank more than twenty Allied vessels in the waters of the St. Lawrence River and the Gulf. Despite the tense situation on the river, tending the lights remained essential to vessel safety. However, it was also necessary to avoid assisting the passage of enemy submarines. The Department of National Defence therefore used coded radio messages to transmit instructions to lightkeepers. Rémi Fergusson, a former keeper of the light at Cap des Rosiers on the Gaspé Peninsula, describes how this took place:

[32] APQ-FMTQ, 2, III, Aids to Navigation, A, 12.3, Île Verte, April 27, 1813.

We used to get radio messages. They gave the codes. They repeated it at 10:30 in the morning, at 2:30 in the afternoon ... it went out at 10:30 at night and at 2:30 in the morning. They said: a notice to lightkeepers, follow instructions "A" for Alpha; then repeated it three times. That meant, keep the lamp lighted ... If they had said "B" for Bravo it would have meant there was danger about, a sub or something. Then we would put out the light and stop the fog horn until new orders came through ... That message was repeated three, four times a day.[33]

In addition to sending out special instructions, the Department of National Defence naturally asked all lightkeepers to be vigilant in contacting them if they ever saw suspect vessels in their area.

Obviously, the strategic position of lighthouse stations made the keepers invaluable intelligence sources in times of war, but the military were not the only ones to take advantage of this situation. By the turn of the century, the fisheries branch also had the cooperation of keepers in its fight against poaching and smuggling. In total, some sixty-five keepers throughout the various lobster-fishing areas of Quebec were advised to report any violations of the regulations governing this type of fishery.[34] The documentation does not reveal whether the keepers actually carried out these orders, nor to what extent they would have done so.

Signal Service

Despite what we have seen so far, the duties connected with lightkeeping were not always of a merely watchful nature. For example, by 1879 some stations also offered a "signal service."[35] The use of new aids to navigation such as semaphore and the telegraph were added to the traditional equipment. These new aids were generally the responsibility of a certified telegraphist, but the keeper or a member of his family could also operate them. In 1902 nineteen light stations were emitting signals along the St. Lawrence River and Gulf shore.[36] The combined use of semaphore and telegraphy was of great service to shipping because it meant that all vessels within the Gulf and the St. Lawrence River could be identified and their progress followed.

Semaphore, a visual signal operated by means of the "International Code of Signals," used eighteen flags *(Figure 21)*. This system of communication was perfected in England in 1855

[33] Interview with Rémi Fergusson, June 19, 1991 (translation).

[34] NAC, RG 12, vol. 1505, no. 7956-9, vol. 1, June 20, 1894; RG 42, C1, vol. 206, no. 33421, April 23, 1917, and September 26, 1921.

[35] Jean Paradis, "Historique de la station de phare du Cap-de-la-Madeleine," internal report, Canadian Coast Guard, Laurentian Region (Quebec, n.d.), 24.

[36] George D. O'Farrell, "Notes on the Lighthouses," 26.

and was quickly adopted by all the world's maritime powers. The head of the Quebec City office of the Department of Marine and Fisheries, J.U. Gregory, provides these details on how it worked:

> The flags represent only the consonants of the alphabet, and by combining two, three or four of these flags and hoisting them together, one can create an arbitrary sign representing words and phrases with the same meaning in all languages …
>
> In combining the flags, a vessel indicates its tonnage, its name, where it is arriving from, or if there is illness aboard. The responding signals will tell the vessel if it is running into danger, is too close to shore, etc.[37]

Each of the stations with signal service also had telegraphy. The information obtained via semaphore was therefore transmitted twice daily to Quebec City via telegraph. The telegraphic

Figure 21.
Semaphore in use at a light station at the turn of the century. The combination of eighteen different flags enabled communication with vessels. The messages were then telegraphed to Quebec City.
(*La Martre Lighthouse Collection, no date*)

---

[37]   J.U. Gregory, *En racontant*, 149 (translation).

messages were eventually published in the newspapers, and in this way shipowners could then be informed of the movements of their vessels.

After the Second World War, semaphore and the telegraph were replaced by the telephone and radiotelephone. Despite this modernization, some keepers were resentful of the extra duties this service entailed, as it required constant vigilance. According to Neil Carré, a former keeper of the Cap au Saumon Light Station, "Everywhere you went you had to take a pencil, paper and binoculars to take down the name of each vessel and the time it passed and report it to Quebec City … that was the real work, and that's what didn't pay."[38] In the 1950s, Carré's father, who had also been a keeper at the Cap au Saumon station, was paid a mere $200 per year for this additional work. Light stations ceased providing this signal service in 1965 when it was taken over by another Coast Guard division.

---

[38]   Interview with Neil Carré, May 13, 1991.

Chapter Four

WORKING CONDITIONS

A ROMANTICIZED VIEW

For most people, light stations are among the most romantic and idyllic places imaginable. Whether we are conscious of it or not, this perception has been instilled in us from a very early age through the works of artists, poets or photographers who were able to take full advantage of the natural beauty of these sites. Basing their perceptions on this stereotype, some people have believed that lightkeepers were very lucky indeed to have a job that brought them into such close communion with nature. Others have gone so far as to think that the lightkeeper's job consisted merely in lighting and extinguishing the beacon, thus enabling him to spend long lazy hours in a magical setting – in a nutshell, heaven on earth.

The former lightkeepers are only too familiar with these clichés – visitors avidly repeated them year in and year out. While some keepers freely admit that they were fortunate to work at exceptional sites – something that certainly cannot be said for all of them – to a man, they all said that their daily routine was very different from the romantic life portrayed by artists.

The keepers would also say that the picture-postcard moments of a sun setting gloriously behind a lighthouse were too often replaced by endless periods of fog, and that at times they had to battle raging seas for days on end without giving any thought to their own health, because that was when their work mattered most.

Some light stations in Quebec were the scenes of tragedies and heroic acts that have never been disclosed. Archival documents reveal that dozens of keepers had to drown before their successors were finally able to obtain more suitable boats. Some lived and worked in appallingly unhealthy conditions, others went mad. Little written material exists regarding these circumstances, and therefore our understanding of the keepers' working conditions has been virtually nonexistent.

TYPES OF LIGHT STATIONS

Before launching into a description of lightkeepers' working conditions, I must provide some clarification regarding the four different types of stations within the Laurentian Region, as the nature of a light station's isolation had a significant impact on its keeper's working conditions. In applying for a posting to one or other of these lighthouses, applicants had little choice but to accept all their drawbacks – after all, "a man's got to feed his family" and employment in the more remote regions was hard to come by.

The stations most prized by keepers were obviously those on the coast located near a village or small community where all the commodities they needed could be found. The keepers and their families could live a life almost as normal as that enjoyed by other community residents. The lights at Pointe des Monts, Cap des Rosiers *(Figure 13)* and Pointe au Père were three typical examples.

Then there were the insular stations such as those located on Anticosti Island, Île Verte *(Figure 14)*, Île Bicquette, Îlet Rouge, Île du Corossol, Île au Marteau, Île aux Perroquets *(Figure 15)*, Bird Rocks and the Magdalen Islands. At these sites, keepers faced harsher living and working conditions, as most of the islands were uninhabited. In addition to the physical isolation, there could be serious problems in obtaining supplies of foodstuffs, firewood and even drinking water. On certain islands, however, keepers could do some hunting and fishing and grow a vegetable garden to meet part of their nutritional needs.

Finally, lightships and pillar lights were among the harshest and most isolated of the Quebec beacons. It is impossible to determine which of the two types was preferred by keepers. In both instances, the living conditions were so severe that families were not permitted to live at these stations, thereby compounding the keepers' isolation. As their name indicates, pillar lights sat on a stonework base entirely surrounded by water. Despite the fact that space was reduced to a bare minimum, these structures at least had the advantage of remaining still, something impossible to achieve on lightships. Pillars at the Upper Traverse, Lower Traverse *(Figure 16)*, Île aux Coudres, Île Blanche *(Figure 17)* and Haut-Fond Prince *(Figure 29)* all fell into this third category. Lightships that were still in operation on the St. Lawrence in the late 1950s included the *Prince Shoal No 7*, at the mouth of the Saguenay; the *Red Islet No 3*, anchored in the same sector near Îlet Rouge, and the *White Island No 20,* off Rivière-du-Loup.

THE KEEPER'S SALARY

In Quebec, like the rest of Canada, lightkeeping was never very well paid. Witness the fact that only a few months before the position completely disappeared from the Laurentian Region in 1988, the pay scale peaked at $30,000 a year. The average salary for the last of the keepers was generally in the neighbourhood of $23,000 to $24,000.[1]

---

[1]   Interview with Lise Cloutier, September 25, 1987.

For a family of four or more in the late 1980s, these wages were certainly not overly generous; yet the salary scale for lightkeepers had increased greatly over the previous decade. According to Donald Graham's study, their average annual salary was a mere $6,500 in 1971, the lowest wages paid to any civil servants at the time.[2]

If these statistics are surprising, it is difficult to imagine how the first lightkeepers in the nineteenth century must have managed. During an 1884 public address in Montreal, William Smith, deputy minister of marine and fisheries, freely admitted that the wages paid to Canadian lightkeepers were very low:

> The salary usually allowed the keeper of a sea coast light is between $300. and $500., and there are often many applicants for any vacancy. The salaries of keepers of river and harbour lights are small, as they generally have opportunities of adding to their income by farming, fishing or some other occupation, in their immediate neighbourhood. At stations where an assistant is necessary, the salary of the keeper is increased to enable him to hire one, but the Government does not appoint him or recognize him in any way.[3]

Mr. Smith was absolutely right. Without the food brought in by fishing, hunting and some farming, a number of lightkeepers would have been unable to provide for their families. In spite of these extra provisions, the administration received many requests from keepers asking for salary increases to keep up with the cost of living. In one of these requests, dated July 7, 1857,[4] the lightkeeper at Île Verte explained that his salary of 125 louis per year had not been increased in twenty years, while the cost of supplies had gone up sharply since 1852. As the father of twelve children, this keeper claimed that he no longer had the means to send the six youngest to school. Numerous other requests from keepers were an indication of the rise in the cost of living in the early 1850s.

ASSISTANTS' SALARIES

Charles Julyan,[5] lightkeeper at Heath Point (Anticosti), stated in 1854 that it was impossible for him to find an assistant for £25, the going annual rate for his station. With salaries generally higher for any other job on the mainland, who would subject himself to the ordeals of such an isolated station for so little money?

---

[2]   Donald Graham, *Lights of the Inside Passage: A History of British Columbia's Lighthouses and Their Keepers* (Madeira Park, B.C.: Harbour Publishing, 1986), 245.
[3]   William Smith, "The Lighthouse System of Canada," a paper … read … 1st Sept. 1884, 18–19.
[4]   APQ-FMTQ, 2, III, Aids to Navigation, A, 12.3, Île Verte, July 7, 1857.
[5]   Ibid., A, 20.3, South Pillar, June 6, 1854.

The issue of salary emerges as one of the worst injustices suffered by assistants in over a century and a half of lightkeeping. It should also be borne in mind that these people received absolutely no recognition from the government until the early 1950s with the forming of a regional lightkeepers' union that supported them in negotiations for national standards. Before that time, the principal keeper was responsible for recruiting assistants and for negotiating conditions related to their lodging, food and salary. A special allowance was paid to the keeper for these purposes.

According to a list of salaries paid by Trinity House in 1861,[6] some assistants received only a third, or at most one half, of the salary granted the principal keeper for an almost identical workload. For example, the keeper at the Belle Isle Light, which was the best-paying station in the Laurentian Region, earned $600 per year, while one of his assistants made only $200. At the South Pillar station off Saint-Jean-Port-Joli and the Îlet Rouge station in the Lower St. Lawrence, keepers earned $500 per year, while their sole assistants earned a paltry $160. The hope of landing a job as principal keeper appears to have been the primary motivation for some assistants. For others, this meagre wage merely augmented the family income when a keeper hired his own son as assistant.

LIVING IN THE TOWERS

In the nineteenth century, the lighthouse tower included rooms to house the keeper and his family. The living conditions were hardly comfortable. Charles Julyan stated:

> I have suffered so much from the severity of the climate during these last two years – especially in the spring when the cold damp Easterly winds are so prevalent that I fear I shall be under the necessity of resigning the charge of the Heath Point Light House in the course of another year or two – and therefore I am anxious to complete the necessary preparation for the removal of my family as soon as possible – which is the only object I have in view in now applying for leave of absence next season.[7]

From this moving testimony of a Heath Point lightkeeper we can gather just how intense the cold could be inside these stone towers built in the first half of the nineteenth century. And, under the administration of Trinity House, six of these towers – at Heath Point, Southwest Point, Pointe des Monts *(Figure 30),* Île Bicquette, Îlet Rouge *(Figures 10 and 22)* and South Pillar – were home to keepers and their families for a number of years. While Charles Julyan

---

6   Ibid., A, 24, "Statements of Light Houses," April 29, 1861.
7   Ibid., A, 1.5, "Anticosti – Heath Point," September 30, 1862.

Figure 22.
Îlet Rouge Light Station, across from the Saguenay, around the turn of the century. In Quebec at least six of these stone towers housed keepers and their families. Their residents often complained of the water leaks, smoke, intense cold and dampness that they had to endure inside these towers.
(Canadian Coast Guard Archives)

appears to have been the only keeper to leave his position because of the cold that permeated his tower, repeated complaints from his colleagues confirm that this type of construction was entirely unhealthy for its occupants.

When the wind blew from the wrong direction over the chimney top, these towers could be filled with smoke in less than fifteen minutes.[8] Keepers had no other choice but to put out the stoves on the various floors of the tower, and in a few hours a bone-chilling cold would take the place of the smoke. Problems with water leaks and dampness were also mentioned frequently. At Pointe des Monts, there was sometimes so much water leaking through from the lantern that the keeper was obliged to remove the beds and take the furniture out of the upper levels of the tower.[9] Such miserable conditions proved almost fatal for the family of Louis-Ferdinand Fafard, fourth keeper at this station in 1872. In the spring of 1873, Fafard wrote the following:

[8]   Ibid., A, 2.5, "Anticosti – South West Point," *c.* 1837.
[9]   Ibid., A, 15.5, "Pointe des Monts," June 25, 1852.

> Toward the end of autumn, with the first heavy snowfall, my family was afflicted with typhoid fever. The onset of this terrible sickness forced seven to their beds, and the rest were soon to follow. I was the only one not abed. My closest neighbour lived twenty miles away, and as bad news is quick to travel far and wide, the lighthouse was soon marked as a site of infection, and even the Indians went out of their way to avoid it in their travels.
>
> … my tending to the light and the invalids was no more than perfunctory when the Lord took pity on us and in His mercy sent us rest and joy by determining that there be a general recovery.[10]

After five years of labouring in that cold, damp tower, Louis-Ferdinand Fafard, like many keepers elsewhere, suffered serious health problems.[11] He was granted six months' leave for treatment at Quebec City, and in the interim his two eldest sons were responsible for tending the light. Six keepers and their families had to put up with the tower's discomforts at Pointe des Monts before the Department of Marine and Fisheries built a suitable dwelling in 1912.

KEEPERS' HOUSES

The stone towers were probably the worst residences that nineteenth-century keepers had to endure. However, complaints from keepers who had separate houses or living quarters adjoining a wooden lighthouse reveal that this accommodation was barely more comfortable than the stone towers.

At the light station on Île Verte in 1817, eleven people had to squeeze into a house that measured only 21 feet by 25.[12] After a number of futile requests to have his house enlarged, Charles Hambelton decided to do the job himself. Trinity House reimbursed him for only two-thirds of the amount he had invested. Robert-Noël Lindsay, second keeper at the Île Verte Light Station, did not mince words about the quality of the construction that went into the second house built for the keeper and his family in 1831:

> I will begin with the roof of the house. It is very badly constructed … The dormers, as well as the roofing around them, have let in much water this autumn …

---

[10]   Faucher de Saint-Maurice, *De tribord à bâbord* (Montreal: Éd. de l'Aurore, 1975), 14 (translation).

[11]   Pierre Frenette, *Le phare historique de Pointe-des-Monts et ses gardiens* (Baie Comeau: Société historique de la Côte-Nord, 1990), 35.

[12]   APQ-FMTQ, 2, III, Aids to Navigation, A, 12.3, Île Verte, April 16, 1818.

The fireplace smokes excessively ... and water comes in between the porch and the house. The passageway joining the house to the tower leaks where it joins both the house and the tower.[13]

And then there were the wretched conditions suffered by the Fraser family at Îlet Rouge, the year after they moved into their house in 1850:

Apart from its small size, I can assure you that seven or eight feet from the stove, water freezes to ice and that in the cupboards, food also freezes. On the 16th of December, therefore, we were obliged to leave this dwelling and take refuge in the tower. I therefore leave it to you, Sir, to judge whether a family of thirteen could have been comfortably housed therein.[14]

Twentieth-century lightkeepers certainly enjoyed much more comfortable living conditions than their predecessors *(Figures 23 to 25)*, but it was not until 1955 that separate houses

Figure 23.
The first and second lighthouses at Matane at the turn of the century. Wooden lighthouses in the nineteenth and twentieth centuries came in a number of different designs. In most cases, the keeper's house was attached to the lighthouse itself.
(Canadian Coast Guard Archives)

---

13   Ibid., December 14, 1831 (translation).
14   Ibid., A, 17.4, Îlet Rouge, March 24, 1851 (translation).

Figure 24.
Cap Gaspé: keeper's house and second lighthouse built in 1893.
(Canadian Coast Guard Archives)

Figure 25.
Keeper's house with lantern on top, Petite Île au Marteau, Mingan Islands.
(Canadian Coast Guard Archives, no date)

were provided for keepers and their assistants at coastal and insular stations[15] *(Figures 31 and 32)*. Until that time, assistants were forced to lodge with the principal keeper, and their families could not live at the station. This restriction frequently made it difficult for principal keepers to recruit assistants, as these junior men found it hard to be separated from their families for long periods of time. This policy had gone unchanged since 1809.

THE WORK WEEK

One aspect of the lightkeeper's job that was never quite clear was the length of his work week. In fact, from 1809 until the mid-1970s, there were no regulations to specify its exact duration.

Once they had been hired, keepers were required to go to their stations and remain there until the end of the shipping season, after which they earned three months' holiday. While three months of vacation time may seem enviable, we should keep in mind that because of bad weather, some stations required up to a fifty-six-hour or even an eighty-four-hour work week for each keeper. Workloads such as these could be attributed to the number of keepers at each station and the weather conditions at the site. Periods of fog could last for more than a week, with keepers taking turns in operating and maintaining the fog signal both day and night.

As the lord and master of his station, the principal keeper was responsible for dividing up the daily watches. For two-man stations, keepers could divide a twenty-four-hour period into two watches of twelve hours or four watches of six hours. Assistants had no recourse if the keeper used his authority to secure the day work for himself. As for night watches, they were abolished in the mid-1970s with the arrival of automation. From that time on, light stations were monitored remotely from various control stations during the night. The keepers' working conditions definitely took a turn for the better once they could finally sleep through the night. However, the first steps towards automation marked the beginning of the end of lightkeeping in Quebec.

---

[15]   Interview with Maurice Thibeault, former president of the Association des gardiens de phare de la Région des Laurentides, April 30, 1991.

Chapter Five

UNIQUE LIVING CONDITIONS

DIFFICULT CROSSINGS

As we saw earlier, in general lightkeepers required written permission in order to be away from their stations. Keepers at insular stations and pillars, and the masters and mates of lightships, however, did not require this permission. They were authorized to make a trip to the mainland approximately once a week in order to stock up on goods or for reasons relating to the proper functioning of the lighthouse. While these crossings were essential for survival, they often exposed keepers to very great dangers:

> I tell you that any man who spends a season here never wants to come back because he is afraid of the boat. I had a good man last year who told me that if I did not have another boat he would not come back. That is why I don't have him this year.[1]

This testimony from a keeper at Îlet Rouge in 1863 illustrates just how difficult the crossings could be in the nineteenth century, and they would remain so for the greater part of the twentieth.

There is no official mortality list for lightkeepers. However, Quebec's Trinity House archives reveal that between 1805 and 1875 there were twelve deaths by drowning, two by exploding powder kegs and one by pulmonary tuberculosis. Drowning was thus the number one killer of lightkeepers, and it was during crossings that such tragic fatalities took place. Following the many drownings between 1860 and 1912, a number of requests were made to the Department of Marine and Fisheries for motor launches for insular stations.[2] In support of their demands, keepers stated that crossings in their sailing craft could sometimes take between eight and ten hours with the current against them; that in the absence of wind some keepers were forced to row single-handedly for seven to eight hours in order to reach dry land; and that in the event of an emergency they might not be able to leave the station at all.[3]

---

[1]   APQ-FMTQ, 2, III, Aids to Navigation, A, 17.4, Îlet Rouge, August 20, 1863 (translation).
[2]   NAC, RG 12, vol. 2126, no. 7952-9, February 10, 1913.
[3]   Ibid.

According to the keepers at insular stations, the drownings were due mainly to the type of craft they were using. These boats were "suitable neither in shape nor size for service in these dangerous waters."[4] In 1913 the minister of marine and fisheries was not at all of the same opinion. In response to the many requests he received, the minister reminded keepers that the boats they were given were usually built according to plans provided by the keepers themselves, and that no official complaint had yet been made about these craft. Despite the credibility of their arguments, the keepers made no headway, except in securing permission to purchase and mount engines in their boats – at their own expense.[5] At that time, and up until 1950, these craft resembled large masted skiffs between 20 and 25 feet long with a 7- to 9-foot beam. Around 1960 the insular stations farthest from the mainland, such as Îlet Rouge and Île Bicquette, were provided with launches with enclosed cabins. As in the past, the keeper was still responsible for the cost, installation and maintenance of an engine if he wanted one. It was not until 1970 that the Department of Transport finally agreed to provide all insular stations with genuinely suitable motor launches *(Figure 26)*.

Figure 26.
Motor launch for use by keepers at the Île Bicquette Light, near Rimouski, around 1980.
(Canadian Coast Guard Archives)

---

[4]   Ibid., February 27 and March 4, 1914.
[5]   Ibid., June 29, 1914.

Risking Their Lives

A number of the later lightkeepers and their families experienced one or more traumatic cross-ings. Robert Kavanagh tells the story of how he almost perished, imprisoned in ice when his boat's engine broke down between Île aux Perroquets and Longue Pointe at Mingan at the close of the shipping season.[6] His voice still charged with emotion, Mr. Kavanagh relates that the situ-ation became so critical that he vowed to the Virgin Mary that he would erect a statue to her at the light station if he and his assistant finished their journey alive. As if by a miracle, a channel opened up behind them and they were able to row back to the station. As promised, there is a statue on Île aux Perroquets commemorating this dramatic voyage. While not all keepers had such close brushes with death as Mr. Kavanagh and his assistant, most will be haunted for many years to come by the memory of some of their crossings.

Anticipate the Worst: The Golden Rule

Keepers at insular stations had to anticipate the worst when it came to supplying their stations with food and fresh water, as weather conditions could on occasion delay crossings for several days. Fishing, hunting and keeping a vegetable garden might meet part of the family's food requirements, but the need for drinking water forced keepers to make frequent crossings.

To solve the fresh water problem, tanks were built in the basements of keepers' houses in the early 1950s. They looked like cement swimming pools and could take up almost half the basement's floor space. Rainwater from the roof was channelled to the tank through a simple network of gutters. According to Maurice Thibeault, former keeper at Île Bicquette, the tanks had some serious drawbacks: for example, the water in them froze at the beginning and end of the shipping season. Furthermore, some keepers suffered from stomach ailments and rashes after drinking the tank water.[7] This problem could be attributed to the fact that in the islands of the St. Lawrence, the rooftops of houses were, and still are, visited by large bird populations.

THE SEASON GETS LONGER

According to Mr. Thibeault, beginning in 1960, four light stations deemed essential to naviga-tion in the Gulf and in the St. Lawrence River remained open and manned by their respective keepers throughout the year. Going from the Gulf towards Quebec City, these were Île du Corossol, Pointe des Monts, Haut-Fond Prince and Îlet Rouge.

---

[6]   Danielle Brie, "L'histoire des phares et de leurs gardiens," radio program *L'aventure*, CBF, Radio-Canada, Montreal, September 1991, cassette 91095.
[7]   Interviews with Maurice Thibeault, April 30, 1991, and with Yvon Desbiens, April 24, 1991.

From then on, all lighthouse lamps along the Gaspé coast from Pointe au Père to Gaspé remained lighted throughout the year. While keepers lived at their station houses year-round, they were only on duty for nine months – from April to December. An electric light with an automatic bulb changer shone permanently through the winter months. The same was true for coastal stations west of the Saguenay to Quebec City.

FAMILY LIFE

Quebec's Trinity House archives reveal almost nothing about the nineteenth-century lightkeeper's family life. However, we do know that in the early days only the principal keeper could have his family live with him at the station; this privilege was only granted to assistants in 1955, when separate housing was made available to them. From our standpoint in the electronic age, it is hard to imagine families living for nine months, or even the entire year, at such Spartan stations as Îlet Rouge or, worse still, the South Pillar. Both were completely devoid of trees, and in the case of the South Pillar off Saint-Jean-Port-Joli, the children's only play area was a hump of rock approximately 1,500 feet long by some 100 feet wide *(Figure 33)*.

There are no words to describe the sense of sacrifice felt by people living under such conditions. The only complaint made by Thomas Roche, second keeper at the South Pillar in 1854, was that he wanted to spend the winter on the mainland.[8] Roche hoped to send his children to school after the shipping season was over. We have no idea whether or not the administrators at the Trinity House of Quebec allowed him this privilege; we do know that this lighthouse had to be tended year-round to avoid vandalism. Charles Julyan, his predecessor, was permitted to leave the islet during the winter, but Trinity House held him responsible for any damage done to the lighthouse.

Schooling

Schooling was a problem for all families at isolated light stations. The wives of keepers often took on the role of teacher, at least for a while, so that the family could stay together. In the case of the West Point station on Anticosti Island, the department appears to have actually hired a teacher to instruct the keeper's twelve children.[9] Still, all these were temporary arrangements. Sooner or later, family members had to resign themselves to sending children to regular school. Some children were boarded out with relatives or friends. Most of the keepers I met with said that school interrupted their family life, as mother and children would have to settle on the

---

[8]   APQ-FMTQ, 2, III, Aids to Navigation, A, 20.3, South Pillar, 1854.
[9]   Interview with Léonard Ouellet, April 29, 1991.

mainland until the next summer vacation. This separation was all the more difficult for keepers because it was compounded by the physical isolation of their stations.

But what about the culture shock that the children must have experienced, children who may never have known an environment other than their light station? Luc Caron, former keeper at Anticosti Island's most isolated station on Heath Point, describes the problems these children faced in adapting to school:

> It sure wasn't easy, especially for number three. For the first days of school she sat on the floor by the door and dared anyone to come near her. That went on until we went to class with her. Then everything fell into place. There was nothing else we could do.[10]

Charles Lindsay, a descendant of the Lindsay dynasty of Île Verte keepers, revealed that his first experience at boarding school, as well as that of his brother and his father before him, came to an early end. He attributes their failure to various factors – boredom, for example, or the difficulty of adapting to a highly regimented life that involved walking in straight lines, waking up at a certain time, and going to mass in the morning. As he so aptly puts it: "It was an uphill battle. The first time we went to boarding school, all three of us failed to make it through a year. I got through two months, Jocelyn one month, and Dad, well, he probably got through a couple of months."[11] Despite rocky academic beginnings, Charles Lindsay went on to become a CEGEP teacher in Rimouski and Jocelyn a professor at the Université Laval in Quebec City.

LIFE ON THE LIGHTSHIPS

A study of the life of lightkeepers would be incomplete if it did not include the role of lightships and their crews. A traditional lighthouse was a perfectly acceptable means of warning ships of the dangers of a rocky coastline, an island or any other major hazard to navigation. However, there had to be another way to deal with less obvious, but often more serious, hazards, those that could easily escape notice during good weather. Such hazards included sandbanks or shoals and reefs that the tide covered with only a few metres of water *(Figure 34)*. It was nearly impossible to build a lighthouse on the unstable foundations in areas like these, making them even more dangerous. In these situations, a lightship was firmly anchored near the hazard to alert mariners to its presence *(Figures 27 and 28)*.

---

[10]   Interview with Luc Caron, May 9, 1991 (translation).
[11]   Interview with Charles Lindsay, May 1, 1991 (translation).

Figure 27.
White Island Reef No 5 lightship, leaving Quebec Harbour in the spring of 1914 for its station near Rivière-du-Loup.
(*Canadian Coast Guard Archives*)

Figure 28.
Some lightships had no means of propulsion. At the close of the shipping season, they were towed to their winter berths in the Bassin Louise at Quebec City.
(*Canadian Coast Guard Archives, no date*)

Lightships

This aid to navigation consisted of a vessel equipped with lights to mark a dangerous sector during the night. During the day, it could not be mistaken for any other vessel because its entire hull was painted red or black and its name was painted in large white letters on each side. Furthermore, it had a fog signal to indicate its presence during storms or in fog. Some lightships, such as the *Red Islet No 3* (stationed off Îlet Rouge), were equipped with engines that enabled them to move under their own power, but most did not, and these had to be towed and then anchored at the correct position. In both cases, however, lightships required crews to see to the maintenance and proper functioning of all the aids to navigation on board. In the 1950s twelve men shared the four six-hour watches on the powered lightships, while only seven manned those ships without propulsion. This difference in number was due to the additional personnel responsible for monitoring and maintaining the engines.

The responsibilities of lightship crews were almost identical to those of lighthouse keepers: each crew member was required to see to the upkeep and proper functioning of all navigational aid equipment. As for working conditions, some would say that life on board the lightships was a great deal more difficult than on a land station. Mr. Esquiros's words, with reference to a lightship in the English Channel, are convincing:

> Experience has shown that a life aboard these vessels is beyond the moral and physical strengths of human nature. The crushing monotony of the same vistas, the sight of the same white-capped waters as far as the eye can see, the sound of every blowing wind and the crashing of the waves that is so resounding that men at times cannot hear each other speak – all this must exert a sinister control over the spirit … What is surprising is that there are men who would face an existence under such harsh conditions; the English themselves have ranked the crew members of light-vessels among the "curiosities of civilization."[12]

Seaman C.-H. Fraser

Quebec had its own "curiosities of civilization" in the seven to eight lightships in service between 1830 and the early 1960s. Charles-Hector Fraser was one of the last seamen to have worked on the Îlet Rouge lightship in 1959. When interviewed, Mr. Fraser admitted that the ship's rolling was one of the worst things he had to put up with: "A ship at anchor is worse than a boat that's moving because when you are under way you can take the wave differently, or even avoid it; but

---

[12]   Louis Figuier, "Les phares," in *Les merveilles de la science* (Paris: Jouvet, 1867–70), vol. 4, 507 (translation).

when you're in a lightship, it just rolls with the waves, which makes it worse."[13] In order to truly appreciate Mr. Fraser's comments, we should remember that during storms these ships were just like corks bobbing anchored in the middle of the ocean. Working on board the lightships, therefore, did not suit every constitution. At least not Charles-Hector Fraser's – he suffered from seasickness. In spite of his handicap, Fraser had to put up with the situation, and it was only after much suffering and misery that he was able to terminate his nine-month contract on the lightship. Others, with stronger stomachs than Fraser's, seem to have adjusted to the unique rolling and pitching of lightships, as they spent more than twenty years of their life on board.[14] However, the documentation does not always reveal their state of health.

Captain D.E. Fraser

Someone who did have sea legs was Captain David E. Fraser, who watched his health deteriorate as the result of a sedentary life on board the lightship *Red Islet No 3*. In an emotional letter written to administrators at the Department of Marine and Fisheries in April 1929,[15] Fraser attributes the decline in his health to an unbalanced diet (there was no refrigerator on board) and lack of exercise; he added that he was under orders to eat a diet of fresh foods. He therefore requested permission to leave the lightship on a regular basis to buy fruit, vegetables and fresh fish. In order to improve his condition, he would also need to go ashore for exercise. Fraser was granted a maximum of ten days' absence a month during the 1929 season.

Shore Leave

The permission secured by Captain Fraser would have made the rest of his men green with envy, as shore leave was very rare for a lightship's crew. The 1873 annual report of the Department of Marine and Fisheries would lead us to believe that it was nonexistent at the end of the nineteenth century.[16]

　　Only the master of a lightship could grant shore leave to members of his crew, he being the only employee recognized by the government. Even then, the master himself was only authorized to leave the vessel in order to secure supplies; any other absence had to be approved by the

---

13　Interview with Charles-Hector Fraser, April 29, 1991 (translation).

14　These were Andrew Christensen and his son, both captains on the lightship *Prince Shoal* stationed at the mouth of the Saguenay on the site of the current pillar at Haut-Fond Prince. Interview with Louis-Joseph Therrien, June 13, 1991.

15　NAC, RG 42, C1, vol. 1047, no. 101-3-2, April 29, 1929.

16　Canada, Parliament, Legislature, *Sessional Papers,* no. 8, Appendix 37, "Annual Report of the Department of Marine and Fisheries 1872" (Ottawa: Queen's Printer, 1873), 349.

department. His contract required him to hire a crew of at least seven men and to feed and pay them from his own salary; it contained no provision for even one day of leave.

Fortunately, working conditions improved somewhat during the twentieth century, and all crew members could hope for a few days of leave during the shipping season. Whether for humanitarian reasons or just because they wanted to hold on to their crews, lightship captains allowed each crew member in turn to accompany them on their trips to resupply the vessel. According to Antoine Therrien, former engineer on board *Prince Shoal No 7* and *Red Islet No 3*, these excursions could last two or even three consecutive days because of violent winds that would prevent the men from returning to the vessel. In total, they might add up to ten days off a year for each member of the crew.[17] One can imagine how those days must have been anxiously awaited, given that the normal shipping season comprised over 250 work days.[18]

The Risk of Collisions

Another factor made living conditions aboard a lightship more uncomfortable: the possibility of being rammed by another vessel. This fear was well founded, as marine accidents were frequent in the nineteenth century. The first lightship in operation below Quebec City, the *Brillant*, was struck head on by the bark *Miramichi* on May 20, 1841.[19] On the other side of the Atlantic, this type of accident culminated in the late 1920s with the lightship *Downs* being sliced in two by the *City of York*. The *Elbe I, Gull, Ambrox* and *South Goodwin* experienced similar fates.[20] The introduction of short-wave radio reduced the risk of these accidents considerably. Nevertheless, Louis-Joseph Therrien, engineer aboard the lightship *Prince Shoal No 7* (at the mouth of the Saguenay), said that despite all the technological advances, crew members on a lightship still felt uneasy when a vessel appeared to be approaching a little too close in the fog.

An Imperfect Aid

Lightships rendered a great service to shipping, but their limitations had to be recognized. By 1860, the chief engineer with the Department of Public Works criticized the vessels for being far less effective and safe than conventional lighthouses, with the pitching and rolling often upsetting their lamps. Furthermore, lightships were notorious for dragging their anchors and even for breaking their chains, literally setting themselves adrift.[21] In such instances, these aids to naviga-

---

17   Interview with Antoine Therrien, May 13, 1991.
18   NAC, RG 42, C1, vol. 1047, no. 101-3-2, 36.
19   APQ-FMTQ, 1, A, Minutes, vol. 6, May 25, 1841, 563.
20   Jean-Paul Dumoutier and René Gast, *Des phares et des hommes* (Paris: Éd. Maritimes J.-C. Lallès, 1985), 128.
21   NAC, RG 11, B1 (a), vol. 230, no. 227, February 28, 1860.

tion became real hazards for mariners because they marked an incorrect route. Finally, the cost of maintaining a lightship was a great deal higher than that for a land-based light, given that a lighthouse could easily be tended by two or three keepers, while a lightship's crew might at times include more than a dozen men.

All of these factors, along with recent technological advances, meant that our last lightships were replaced in the 1960s by automatic buoys and by pillar lights such as the one at Haut-Fond Prince at the mouth of the Saguenay.

LIFE ON THE PILLAR LIGHTS

The isolation and solitude on a pillar light, combined with the absence of spouse and children, often led to tensions running high between individuals whose personalities might not always be compatible. In a notarized document dated July 8, 1858, Louis Lemieux, one of the assistants at the Cap des Rosiers station, claimed that the principal keeper had threatened before witnesses to smash his head in with an axe.[22] Obviously the keeper must have been carried away to have said that, but it would be safe to assume that similar threats were fairly frequent on the pillar lights, especially when most of the keepers who worked on them still maintain today that the climate was fraught with conflict, disagreements and tension.

The isolation of coastal *(Figure 35)* or insular stations was nothing compared to the isolation felt on pillar lights *(Figure 36)*. On these concrete or metal structures, it was out of the question to grow a little vegetable garden, hunt, or even fish because the currents were much too swift. What could the men do to relieve the boredom when their watch was over? Go out on the turret? Only if the weather permitted. On the pillars, the wind blows almost continually and often so violently that it is virtually impossible to stay upright *(Figure 37)*. In rough weather, keepers had to stay indoors – sometimes for up to ten days. According to Léonard Ouellet, who worked on the Île Blanche Pillar for seventeen years, the lack of physical activity was the worst hardship for keepers tending this type of light:

> So we used to go around the thing two, three times. But once you went around two, three times, there wasn't much to it. You look at the islands over there and say, God, it'd be great to get to that island and go for a walk in the woods – hike in the woods. When you could see fall coming – there was no more getting out, we were stuck for two months. There was nothing to do on that thing, and eventually you'd get stiff. I think that was the toughest part.[23]

---

[22] APQ-EMTQ, 2, III, *Aids to Navigation,* A, 8.4, "Cap-des-Rosiers," July 8, 1858.
[23] Intervuew with Léonard Ouellet, April 29, 1991 (translation).

Figure 29.
Haut-Fond Prince Pillar Light off Tadoussac, in the late 1970s.
(Photo: D. Chamard, Canadian Coast Guard)

Figure 30.
**Pointe des Monts Light on the North Shore, in 1990. This structure, now finished in clapboard, was the
last stone tower lived in by its keeper in Quebec. In 1912 the keepers moved into the adjoining house.**
(Photo by the author)

Figure 31.
House of keeper and his assistant, Escarpment Bagot Light Station, Anticosti Island.
(Canadian Coast Guard Archives, no date)

Figure 32.
Assistant's house (left) and principal keeper's house (right), Cap de Bon-Désir Light Station east of Tadoussac, in 1990. It was not until 1955 that the families of keepers and their assistants would enjoy separate housing.
(Canadian Coast Guard Archives)

Figure 33.
South Pillar or Stone Pillar west of Saint-Jean-Port-Joli, in the 1980s. Stationed on this small rocky islet,
the keeper and his family endured a particularly harsh life.
(Canadian Coast Guard Archives)

Figure 34.
Pillar lights at the Cap Brûlé Range near Sainte-Anne-de-Beaupré. By the nineteenth century, lightships
were being anchored near sandbanks, reefs and shoals to mark these most deceptive hazards for shipping.
In the following century, they were replaced with pillar lights.
(Canadian Coast Guard Archives, no date)

Figure 35.
Some coastal stations, like the one at Cap au Saumon, west of Saint-Siméon,
were fairly isolated, with no access roads at all.
(Canadian Coast Guard Archives, no date)

Figure 36.
Haut-Fond Prince Pillar off Tadoussac. The isolation of coastal or insular stations was nothing compared to the isolation of the pillars.
(Canadian Coast Guard Archives, no date)

Figure 37.
Île Blanche Pillar Light off Cacouna, around 1980. The wind blew almost continually on the pillars, and the keepers were sometimes forced to stay indoors for days at a time, with no chance even to go out on the gallery.
(Canadian Coast Guard Archives)

Figure 38.
Beginning in the 1970s, keepers at the Île Blanche Pillar were relieved in teams of two by helicopter every fifteen days.
(Canadian Coast Guard Archives, 1992)

Families were not allowed on the pillars because of the particularly harsh conditions. Beginning in the 1970s, keepers on the pillar light at Île Blanche were relieved by helicopter every two weeks by another team of two men throughout the year *(Figure 38)*. Prior to the 1970s, there were no more relief crews as of September because of the bad weather. All of the keepers had to stay on the pillars until the Christmas season. Fortunately, a radio-telephone system allowed them to remain in contact with their families. A call was routed through the station at Pointe Noire, across from Tadoussac, and the keeper at that station retransmitted the call to the family on shore. A ten-minute call per week was paid for by the Coast Guard for each of the pillar keepers. The arrival of the first CB radios in the 1970s meant that the isolation of keepers on the pillars was somewhat reduced. Beyond that, do-it-yourself projects and amateur radio were their main sources of entertainment.

WHEN THE FORCES OF NATURE EXPLODE

All lightkeepers on the St. Lawrence and in the Gulf have witnessed particularly violent storms at their stations. While most escaped more frightened than hurt, others barely survived the hellish nightmares unleashed when the elements vented their fury on the station – even resulting in death for one of their own.

Wind

Faucher de Saint-Maurice describes the tragedy that took place at the light station on St. Paul Island, off the coast of Cape Breton, on August 16, 1876. This excerpt from the keeper's official report, as quoted by Faucher de Saint-Maurice, speaks for itself:

> Suddenly, I think it was about 9:30, I heard a terrible noise; and turning toward it, I saw a sight that made me shake from head to toe. Less than a quarter of a mile away from where I stood I saw, toward the west, rocks, dirt, water and trees twisting up over a hundred feet into the air. I carefully watched the twister to see which way it was going and realized in terror that it was coming across the cove towards me and was probably going to carry away the house in its raging path.[24]

The keeper continues this incredible story by saying that one of his assistants who was in a field was evidently killed and carried 300 feet away by the tornado. The material damage was extensive:

---

[24]   Faucher de Saint-Maurice, *De tribord à bâbord* (Montreal: Éd. de l'Aurore, 1975), 247 (translation).

> I realized that five buildings had been destroyed, along with their contents, and there wasn't a scrap left. The cabin on the boat, the provision depot and the house are still standing, but terribly damaged; the house is truly in ruins ... The buildings that were destroyed were a shelter, the barn, stable and two other buildings located at the top of the hill 600 feet apart ... The two bridges that I had just crossed an instant before were tossed 400 feet and shattered.[25]

Storms

An equally tragic event occurred at the Point Heath station on Anticosti Island in the 1940s. Marcel Duguay, former keeper at this station, tells the story of a previous keeper whose son died of suffocation during a violent storm a few days before Christmas. And because troubles never seem to come one at a time, the child's mother went mad when she learned the news:

> Anxious to avoid having the mother become hysterical, the courageous father dragged the body of his son, which he had found near the lighthouse, to the powder magazine. He explained his son's absence to his wife by saying that her boy would be back in the spring after the wood-cutting season. He had to wait until spring to hand over the poor boy's body to the naval authorities. Upon learning the news, the mother lost her mind.[26]

Waves

A little more recently, on December 25, 1966, the three keepers on the pillar at Haut-Fond Prince at the mouth of the Saguenay experienced a horrifying Christmas when a violent storm, probably the worst in the history of the St. Lawrence, pounded against their light and raged about them for more than thirty-six hours.[27] Designed to withstand twenty-five-foot waves, the pillar was subjected to a repeated onslaught of waves reaching forty-two feet.

The storm was so violent that two doors of one-inch-thick steel, reinforced with iron locks and two-inch beams, were literally smashed in by the force of the waves. These doors were two of the three emergency exits located at Level 51, or fifty-one feet above the pillar base. This was even more alarming for the keepers because this point was thirteen feet higher than the

---

[25]   Ibid. (translation).

[26]   Rodrigue Gignac, "Hiverner dans un phare," *Cap-aux- Diamants*, no. 24 (Winter 1991), 23 (translation).

[27]   The information regarding this storm was drawn from Léon Bernard, "Un Noël terrible au large de Tadoussac," *Le Magazine Maclean*, vol. 8, no. 1 (January 1968), 16–17, 29–32.

highest tide level ever recorded for that sector; however, the infernal and incessant noise of the generators prevented the men from hearing what was going on at the base of the pillar.

Far from calming down, the storm grew worse, and at around eight in the morning, there were forty-two-foot waves pounding against the concrete wall at the level of the living quarters. The first window caved in and each subsequent wave flooded the floor a bit more. With the rising tide, the water came in through the emergency doors and was forced inside up to Level 64, where it disabled the heating system. The situation then became a great deal more serious, and the keepers decided to send out their first distress call:

> There's a terrible storm at the Pillar. A window was smashed in by the waves. The water is coming in like a river through Door 51. The floors are flooded. The heating is out. The pipes have been ripped out. Call Quebec City. The Pillar is shaking so much that it's frightening. Our lives are in danger. If it falls over...[28]

This message was picked up by Jos. Therrien, keeper at the Pointe Noire station, who had had the bright idea of taking his radio-telephone with him to Tadoussac. With great difficulty he managed to get hold of Captain Gaudreau, federal agent for the Port of Quebec. Unfortunately, the bad weather prevented any immediate rescue and the keepers had to wait until 3:30 p.m. on December 26 before being evacuated by helicopter. As Léon Bernard so aptly puts it: "For Claude Fraser, Yvanhoé Gagnon and Roger Lagacé, Santa Claus came by helicopter – 36 hours late."[29]

The material damage left behind by this storm was extensive:

> The living quarters are a mass of debris. On the east side, there are no more walls between the bedrooms and the pillar wall is nothing but a gaping hole open to the river ... In the tower and on the platform, Roger Lagacé noted that the tower's joints had been ripped apart, that $5/8''$ screws had popped out, and that the girders used for climbing from the bottom of the pillar to the top are twisted.[30]

In addition, the powerful xenon lamps of 32 million candlepower each, as well as the 500-watt incandescent lamps, were ripped from their supports and thrown onto the turret floor under the impact of the waves. Keepers Gagnon, Fraser and Lagacé will never forget December 25, 1966.

---

[28]   Ibid., 30 (translation).
[29]   Ibid., 32 (translation).
[30]   Ibid. (translation).

Chapter Six

AUTOMATION

T he nationwide program for automating light stations began in the early 1970s.[1] Canadian Coast Guard administrators saw this program as the response to increasingly urgent petitions for a better quality of life for lightkeepers. In addition, automation seemed to be an ideal solution to the many problems involved in operating and resupplying isolated stations.

KEEPERS' DEMANDS

Among the primary demands made by keepers in the 1960s was the forty-hour work week. After completing their week, keepers hoped to be able to leave their stations for a brief break. This request posed a serious problem for the Coast Guard. For safety reasons, it did not want a keeper to be left alone at an isolated site. At stations tended by two men, therefore, the forty-hour work week could not apply. Following a number of confrontations between the administration and the keepers' union, the Department of Transport made the decision to go ahead with automation and the Laurentian Region was designated the "pilot region" for testing the dependability of the new equipment.

A PILOT REGION

The choice of the Laurentian Region as the pilot region in the automation process was supported by a variety of factors. First, this region had a number of isolated lighthouses. Second, its lights were spread out over a wide area, with the region covering both shores of the St. Lawrence up to the lower North Shore and the Gaspé Peninsula. And finally, the technicians in this region were the best trained at the time to effect this significant technological change.

By the early 1970s, eight of the twenty-nine manned stations in the pilot region were automated. Fortunately, this decision did not mean job losses for any of the keepers, as the Coast

---

[1] Interview with Lise Cloutier, September 25, 1987.

Guard timed the changes to coincide with voluntary retirements or with transfers to other stations. The first automation trials were so successful that the Department of Transport proposed expanding its program to the national level. By 1975 the project was approved by the Canadian Treasury Board and the funds necessary for its implementation were made available to each of the Canadian Coast Guard administrative regions.

THE KEEPERS LEAVE THE LIGHTS

In the meantime, lightkeepers in the Laurentian Region had no other choice but to stoically watch the installation of batteries of electronic equipment over which they had no control, and which, sooner or later, would replace them. It was obviously a blow to their pride and incentive when all the duties specific to lightkeeping were handed over to machines that fulfilled them perfectly and, what's more, without the slightest fatigue. Our lightkeepers were certainly completely aware of the fact that they could not stand in the way of progress, but at the same time, not one of them was truly resigned to giving up the lightkeeping that represented his entire life.

According to Department of Transport projections, from 1981 on, all lighthouses west of Pointe au Père were to be automated; the following year, all those along the North Shore and the Gaspé Peninsula would follow suit. Finally, one year after the automation of a station, its position of lightkeeper would be abolished. As might be expected, this timetable prompted strong reactions from the keepers' union and it also sparked a real controversy in the four other Department of Transport administrative regions. Faced with this opposition, the management of the Laurentian Region opted to slow down its automation program, which was not finalized in Quebec until 1988. The stations at Haut-Fond Prince and Îlet Rouge, both at the mouth of the Saguenay, were the two last manned stations in Quebec.

Chapter Seven

CONCLUSION

A VITAL ROLE

Lightkeeping, although an unassuming and misunderstood profession throughout its 179-year history in Quebec, was nevertheless essential to the economic development of Canada. After all, was it not by way of the St. Lawrence River, from whose most dangerous hazards the lighthouses were to protect mariners, that the history of our country began? How many of those vessels loaded with goods and carrying colonists, priests, administrators, soldiers, immigrants, merchants or visitors – how many hundreds, or even thousands – owe their safety to the vigilance of those solitary lookouts that were our lightkeepers? No one will ever be able to answer that question, and that is precisely one of the most frustrating aspects of lightkeeping. Over the years, we even came to forget that behind all those lights there were men, men who for the most part had been trained by their fathers to the hard life of a lightkeeper. To the detriment of their own health, these men ensured that their lights burned every night and that their station's fog signals never ceased sounding in fog and storms, because that was just when they were needed most.

Although extremely demanding, this position offered very little in return to those who filled it. While some men felt an almost complete sense of freedom on their stations, all were driven by an unfailing love of the sea. And if their freedom seems to us entirely relative, their love of the sea was truly exceptional. No one can remain indifferent when they describe the sense of complicity they felt with this powerful and unpredictable friend. Some keepers say that they could spend hours watching the sea, and it is this daily contact with the sea that they appear to miss most since their retirement from the lighthouses. After so many years in the front rows of such a spectacular show, they cannot hide the strong feelings that might be disguised by their actual words. However, progress is unstoppable, and lightkeepers along the St. Lawrence River and the Gulf have had to resign themselves to the disappearance of their way of life.

IN THE FINAL ANALYSIS

This great river, the St. Lawrence, whose dangers were the dread of seamen in the eighteenth and nineteenth centuries, was finally tamed through the addition and improvement of aids to navigation. These aids have become highly sophisticated in recent years. While it is true that fully automated electronic equipment replaced keepers at light stations in the late 1980s, much more accurate aids to navigation have emerged in the last decade.

The very latest in navigation equipment is the GPS, or Global Positioning System. Originally designed for military purposes by the U.S. Defense Department, this system became accessible worldwide in 1983. It works through the reception of satellite signals that enable a vessel to determine its position. The GPS is accurate to approximately 100 metres, but a recent improvement to the system, the DGPS – Differential Global Positioning System – has brought the margin of error down to less than 10 metres. The Canadian Coast Guard is the agency responsible for providing this DGPS service in Canada, and the installation of the system here is slated for completion in 1997.

Similar technological developments have made it practically impossible to mistake the location of vessels on the River or Gulf of St. Lawrence. Human error is always a possibility, and instruments do break down and vessels do have mechanical failures; however, in recent times, marine accidents or incidents have become increasingly rare.

LOOKING TOWARDS THE FUTURE

As to the future of light stations, they will remain in service for safety reasons, in spite of their outdated technology. These aids to navigation are now viewed as a last resort when electronic instruments on board vessels fail. Soon, all light stations in the Laurentian Region will be powered by solar energy, another way that maintenance costs can be reduced. However, given the incredible progress in electronics, no one can guess how lighthouses will be used in the coming decades.

AN INVITATION

Over the last few years, a number of lighthouses on the St. Lawrence and in the Gulf have added an educational slant to their roles as aids to navigation. In the Lower St. Lawrence and Gaspé Peninsula areas, visitors are invited to view various exhibitions or take guided tours at the lighthouses at Pointe au Père, La Martre, Cap des Rosiers and Cap Gaspé. Along the North Shore, similar activities are also offered to the public at the stations at Pointe des Monts, Cap de Bon-Désir and Pointe Noire. It is therefore to be hoped that these proud towers of stone or concrete will stand in memory of their keepers for many years to come.

APPENDIX A

Distinguishing Characteristics of the Lighthouses under the Charge of the Trinity House of Quebec, from Portneuf to the Strait of Belle Isle, 1809-1862

BELOW QUEBEC CITY

Name of Lighthouse	Year	Position	Order of Light	Number of lamps and reflectors	Colour	Fixed or revolving	Fuel	Height of light centre above high water (feet)	Miles seen in fine weather	Type of construction	Height in feet of the building — Diameter (feet) top/base
Green Island (Île Verte)	1809	Pointe à Michaud at the north end of the island	Catoptric	13	White	Fixed	Porpoise and wolffish oil	60	14	Circular stone tower, with clap-boarding painted white	40 18/24
Pointe-des-Monts	1830	Approx. 1/4 mile north-east of the point	1st order lantern, catoptric	17	White	Fixed	"	90	15	"	90 20/30
Lightship *Brillant*	1830	Northeast entrance of the Traverse St-Roch-des-Aulnaies	Catoptric	16 one lantern per mast	White	Fixed	"	100	10	Two masted schooner, 69 ft by 22 ft beam	21 draught
Anticosti	1831	Southwest Point	1st order lantern, catoptric	21	White	Revolving: one complete revolution every 3 minutes: 1 minute between flashes	"	110	16	Conical stone tower with clap-boarding painted white	75 26/36
Heath Point, Anticosti	1836	Southeast point	1st order lantern, catoptric	17	White	Fixed	"	110	15	"	90
Biquet Island (Isle Bicquette)	1843	West point	1st order lantern, catoptric	21	White	Revolving: one complete revolution every 6 minutes; 2 minutes between flashes	Porpoise and wolffish oil	112	17	Circular lime-stone tower	65 18/22

APPENDIX A (cont'd)

Name of Lighthouse	Year	Position	Order of Light	Number of lamps and reflectors	Colour	Fixed or revolving	Fuel	Height of light centre above high water (feet)	Miles seen in fine weather	Type of construction	Height in feet of the building Diameter (feet) top/base
South Pillar or Stone Pillar	1843	50 fathoms off the southern point of the islet	Catoptric	15	White	Revolving: one complete revolution in 1 min. 30 seconds	Porpoise and wollfish oil	68	13	Circular limestone tower with 3 raised horizontal stone cordons	52 17½/22
Red Island (Isle Rouge)	1848	Southwest shore	Catoptric	24	Red	Fixed	"	75	12	"	51 19½/26
Belle Isle	1858	Extreme soutwest point of island	1st order lantern, dioptric	1 lamp with 5 burners	White	Fixed	"	470	28	Circular stone tower with facing of white firebrick	62
Point Amour	1858	Southeast point of Baie de Forteau	2nd order lantern, catadioptric	1 lamp with 5 burners	White	Fixed	"	155	18	"	109½ 17'6"/25'9"
Anticosti	1858	Extreme west point	2nd order lantern, catadioptric	1 lamp with 5 burners	White	Fixed	"	112	15	"	109½ 17'6"/25'9" 112 17/25½
Cape Rosiers (Cap Rosier)	1858	East coast of Gaspé Peninsula, extreme point of cape	1st order lantern, catadioptric	1 lamp with 5 burners	White	Fixed	"	136	16	"	
Father Point (Pointe-au-Père)	1859	On the point, County of Rimouski	Catoptric	6	Red	Fixed	Coal oil (kerosene)	43	10	Octagonal white wooden tower	46
Bellechasse	1862	Island's extreme north-west point	Catoptric	5	White	Fixed	"	64	10	Square wooden tower	29½
Crane Island (Île aux Grues)	1862	Island's southeast coast	Catoptric	5	White	Fixed	"	48 low water	10	Octagonal wooden tower	42
Grande île de Kamouraska	1862	Island's northeast point	Catoptric	?	White	Fixed	"	162	12	Square wooden tower	36½
Long Pilgrim (Long Pèlerin)	1862	West of island's centre	4th order lantern, catadioptric	1	White	Fixed	?	212	12	Circular brick tower	39
Brandypot Islands (Île du Pot à l'Eau de Vie	1862	Southeast extremity of southern island	4th order lantern, dioptric lens	1	White	Fixed	?	78	10	Circular fire-brick tower	39

APPENDIX A (cont'd)

ABOVE QUEBEC CITY

Name of Lighthouse	Year	Position	Order of Light	Number of lamps and reflectors	Colour	Fixed or revolving	Fuel	Height of light centre above high water (feet)	Miles seen in fine weather	Type of construction	Height in feet of the building Diameter (feet) top/base
Sainte-Croix	1842	South shore at high water mark, $^1/2$ mile north of church	Catoptric	2	White	Fixed	Porpoise and wolffish oil, from 1863: coal oil (kerosene)	38	6	Wooden tower painted white	33
Port-Neuf	1843	Two lighthouses, North Shore	Catoptric	2	White	Fixed	"	90	5	Stone	25
		South Shore	Catoptric	2	White	Fixed	"	208	5	Wooden	23
Saint-Antoine	1855	South Shore	Catoptric	2	White	Fixed	"	33	6	Wooden tower painted white	20

Source: APQ-FMTQ, 1, A, Minutes, vol. 11: "Statement of the number, position and distinguishing characteristics of the light houses under the charge of the Trinity House of Quebec in the Gulf and River St. Lawrence (February 5, 1861)," 373–74; in Jean Leclerc, *Le Saint-Laurent et ses pilotes: 1805–1860* (Montreal: Leméac, 1991), 208–19 (translation).

APPENDIX B

Statement Showing the Number of Vessels Wrecked and Stranded in the Gulf and
River St. Lawrence, 1840–1849 and 1856–1866

DATE		NAME OF VESSEL	AT WHAT PLACE
YEAR	MONTH		
1840	April	Magnet	White Island Reef
		Hibernia	North Pilgrim
	May	Hero	Southwest of Anticosti
		Voyageur	Bonaventure
		Chippewa	Cape Rosier
		Arabian	ditto
		Brothers	Percé Rocks
	June	Eleanor	Hare Island Shoal
		Union	The Traverse (St. Rochs)
		Minerva	Beaumont
		Mountaineer	Cacouna
	July	Quebec	Manicouagan Shoals
		England	Coming up the river
		Cerus	Anticosti
	October	Three schooners	Grand River
	December	Marie Charlotte	Magdalen Islands
		Brig	ditto
1841	May	A bark	Bic
		ditto	Anticosti
		Annandale	Magdalen Islands
	June	Aleutheria	Rivière Ouelle
		Orwin	Green Island
	July	Fair Isle	Anticosti
		Waimsley Dale	ditto
		Townley	ditto
	August	Undaunted	Sable Island
		Lord Cochrane	Labrador
	September	Margaret	Egg Island
		Quebec	Red Island Reef
		Two vessels	Anticosti
		Full-rigged ship	Métis
	October	Helen Stewart	Crane Island
		Caroline	Beaumont Reef
	November	Portland	Ste. Anne
		Eddystone	St. Thomas Shoal

APPENDIX B (cont'd)

DATE		NAME OF VESSEL	AT WHAT PLACE
YEAR	MONTH		
1842	May	Jane Black	Pointe des Monts
		Kent	Seven Islands
		Courier	Métis
		Morning Star	Duncan Reef
	September	Euphrosine	Matane
		Adelaide	Ste. Marguerite Island
		Resolution	Matane
	October	Argyle	Cape Breton
	November	Welsford	Green Island
		George Ramsay	Cacouna
		Briton	Green Island
		Gleaner	Goose Island
		Aberdeen	Green Island
		Enterprize	Manicouagan Shoals
		Alderman Thompson	Anticosti
		Emerentine	ditto
	December	Bellona	Kamouraska
		Thetis	Manicouagan Shoals
		Johanna	Heron, Baie des Chaleurs
1843	April	Brunette	St. Paul's Island
		Quebec	Red Island Reef
	May	Bachelor	West Point, Island of Orleans
		William Ripon	St. Paul's Island
		Tom Moore	White Island Reef
	September	African	Cape St. Lawrence
	November	Content	Caribou Island
		Josephine	Jeremie Island
		Neptune	ditto
		Bernard	ditto
		Mersey	Portneuf
		Crusader	Cape Wapitongane
1844	April	Amaranth	Lost in the Gulf
	May	St. Patrick	Indian Harbour
		Prince Albert	In the Gulf
	July	Hannagh	Anticosti
		Warrior	Magdalen Islands
	October	Indian Chief	Cape Rosier
		Maria (schooner)	Godbret
		A schooner	Godbout
		Quebec	Hare Island
		Orbit	Red Island
		Carleton	Manicouagan Shoals
	November	Cyrus	Portneuf
		Prince George	Ste. Anne

APPENDIX B (cont'd)

DATE		NAME OF VESSEL	AT WHAT PLACE
YEAR	MONTH		
1845	April	Eliza Ann	In the ice (Gulf)
	May	Vanguard	St. Paul's Island
		Rhydiol	In the ice (Gulf)
		Lamport	Cape Breton
		Rosebank	Scatterie
		Sapphire	Cape North Bay
		Thomas & Mary	In the ice
		Amelian	ditto
	June	Coquette	Magdalen Islands
		William Henry	Miquelon
		Indemnity	Magdalen Islands
		Green House	Anticosti
	August	Dumfriesshire	ditto East Point
		Osprey	ditto S.W. Point
	September	Briton's Queen	Flat Island
	October	Eliza Ann	Cape Chat
		Leo	Straits Belisle
	November	Anne Crossman	Rivière Ouelle
		European	Mille Vaches
		Antelope	Ste. Anne
		Gaspé Packet	Red Island
		Reaper	Mille Vaches
		Magnet	Green Island
		Queen	Dog Island
		Elizabeth Atkinson	Manicouagan Shoals
		Covenanter	Goose Island
		Universe	Brandy Pots
		Maria	Crane Island
		Crusader	Kamouraska
		Jane	St. André
		Sir Robert Peel	Kamouraska
		Ceylon	Bic
	December	William Bayard	Cape Chat
		Montreal	ditto
		A schooner	Cape Chat
		Industry	Pilgrim Islands
		Jane Morrison	Manicouagan Shoals
		Stedfast	Magdalen Islands
		Arethusa	ditto
		Ann	Point St. Denis
		William	Portneuf
		Sir Richard Jackson	Manicouagan Islands
		William Lloyd	Magdalen Islands
		Laurel	Green Island
		Elizabeth	Water-logged, and seen passing Gaspé

APPENDIX B (cont'd)

DATE		NAME OF VESSEL	AT WHAT PLACE
YEAR	MONTH		
1846	April	Athol	St. George's Bay
		St. Andrew	Red Island Reef
		Indian Queen	Battures off Cocagne
		A vessel	Water-logged off St. Pierre, Newfoundland
	May	ditto	On the banks
		Pekin	Cape Rosier
		Eagle	Matane
	June	Salisbury	Brandy Pots
		Providence	Portneuf
		Brig	St. Thomas
		Liverpool	Basque Island
		Montreal Packet	Labrador
	July	Lord John Russell	Cape Gaspé
		Wellington	Grand Métis
		Lady Peel	Basque Island
		Borneo	Lost in the Straits of Belle-île
	August	Calcutta	Little Métis
	September	Kate	Goose Island
		Hebe	Manicouagan Shoals
		China	ditto
		Sir James McDonald	Kamouraska Island
		Hartland	Traverse (St. Rochs)
		St. Andrew	Beauport Shoals
		Harvey	Beauport Shoals
		Promise	Point St. Laurent
		Clyesdale	Mille Vaches
		A bark	ditto
		Robert Stride	Green Island
		Cove	Red Island
	October	Industry	The Banks
		Agnes	Pillar Rocks
		Thomas	Mille Vaches
		Magnet	Anticosti
		Milliner	Métis
		Ocean	ditto
		A schooner	Malbaie
		ditto	ditto
	November	Beaver	Miramichi
		Douchfour	Cape Rosier
		Mersey	Matane
		Reliance	ditto
		Empire	ditto
		574	Anticosti
		Countess of Durham	Jeremie Island
		Marquis of Wellesley	St. Simon
		Lloyds	Ste. Anne
		Amy Ann	Cape Chat

APPENDIX B (cont'd)

DATE		NAME OF VESSEL	AT WHAT PLACE
YEAR	MONTH		
1847	May	Rory O'More	Métis
		Geddie	Matane
		Garrick	Cape Rosier
	June	Sylvia	Magdalen Islands
		Miracle	ditto
		Lucius Carey	Gut of Canso
	July	John and Mary	Southwest Point, Anticosti
		Faugh a Ballagh	Brion Island, near Magdalen Islands
		Waterloo	Anticosti
	August	City of Derry	Bicquet Island
		Elizabeth	Jedore
		Canton	Cape Wrath
		Emerald	Cape North
	September	Leo	Ingonish Bay
		Mary Leonore	Fox River
	October	Schooner	ditto
		ditto	ditto
		Princess Charlotte	Trinity Bay
		Mary and Margaret	Blanc Sablon
		Nautilus	ditto
1848	May	The Margaret Pollock	St. Michel
		Astoria	Little Fox River
		Primrose	Southwest Point, Anticosti
		Lumley	English Point
	June	Lady Seaton	Magdalen Islands
		Pekin	Kamouraska
		Effingham	Jeremie Island
	August	William Wallace	Magdalen Islands
	September	A vessel	Anticosti
		2 schooners	Fox River
		A brig	Point Gaspé
		Ann	Anticosti
		Spalpeen	Cape Rosier
		Florence	ditto
	November	Wilson Kennedy	Gaspé

APPENDIX B (cont'd)

DATE		NAME OF VESSEL	AT WHAT PLACE
YEAR	MONTH		
1849	April	Chieftain	Sunk near Bird Islands
	May	Coverdale	Between St. Paul's and Bird Islands
		Gleaner	Bird Islands
		Maria	Near St. Paul's in the ice
		Torrance	ditto
		Mary Elizabeth	In the ice
	June	Resolution	ditto
		Albion	Brion Island
		Veloce	Going into Richibucto
	August	Elizabeth	Brion Island
	September	Blonde	Sable Island
		Lavinia	Grand Pabos
		Marie Louise	Malbaie
		Despatch	English Point
	October	Eldon	Kamouraska
		Sir Charles Napier	Mingan Island
		Elspeth	Labrador
		Eldorado	Red Island
		Queen Victoria	Mille Vaches Shoals
		Lermick	Manicouagan Shoals
		Agnes and Ann	Anticosti
		Mary and Harriett	ditto
	November	Dickson	Cacouna
		St. Lawrence	Miscou Island
		Ste. Helene	Arichat
		Henry Thomas	Gut of Canso

**Number of Lost, Wrecked, Stranded and Damaged Vessels, Voyaging to and from
the Port of Quebec, for the Years 1856 to 1866, Inclusive**

1856	38
1857	49
1858	51
1859	52
1860	43
1861	102
1862	94
1863	75
1864	55
1865	48
1866	67

Source: Canada, *GRCPW 1867* (Ottawa: Hunter Rose and Lemieux, 1868), Appendix 53, 426–28 (translation).

APPENDIX C

Requirements for the Position of Lightkeeper in Canada in 1869

Regulations *for the admission of Light Keepers into the Service of the Dominion of Canada.*

APPLICANTS are required to be of the age of Eighteen years and not above Fifty, and to produce the following certificates:—

Certificate of Birth or other evidence of age.

Certificate from a Medical Man as to present state of health, and particularly whether there is any defect of Eye-sight or inability to distinguish colour.

Certificate of former employment or Trade; if married or single; and if any family.

Certificate of ability to work and properly manage an open Boat.

Certificate of character from last Employer.

Certificate from Schoolmaster or Clergyman of being able to read and write, and of having a fair knowledge of Arithmetic, also of good moral character.

Any deviation from the Regulations above mentioned must be specially brought under the notice of the Minister of Marine and Fisheries, for his sanction and approval.

DEPARTMENT OF MARINE AND FISHERIES,
Ottawa, 1st March, 1869.

Source: APQ-FMTQ, 2, III, Aids to Navigation, A, 25.1, "Admission et conduite des gardiens" (Admission and Conduct of Keepers), March 1, 1869.

ACRONYMS AND ABBREVIATIONS

NAC   National Archives of Canada
APQ-FMTQ   Archives of the Port de Quebec; Fonds de la Maison de la Trinité de
                    Québec (Trinity House of Quebec Holdings)
RCCA   *Report Concerning Canadian Archives*
RAPQ   *Rapport de l'archiviste de la province de Québec*
GRCPW 1867   *General Report of the Commissioner of Public Works, 1867*

BIBLIOGRAPHY

Bayfield, Henry Wolsey et al.
Sailing Directions for the Gulf and River of St. Lawrence. London: Hydrographic Office, 1843.

Sailing Directions for the Island of Newfoundland and Adjacent Coast of Labrador. London: James Imray and Son, 1862.

Bernard, Léon
"Un Noël terrible au large de Tadoussac." *Le Magazine Maclean,* vol. 8, no. 1 (January 1968), 16–17, 29, 32.

Bouchette, Joseph
The British Dominions in North America; or a Topographical and Statistical Description of the Provinces of Lower and Upper Canada. London: Longman, Rees, Orme, Brown, Green and Longman, 1832.

Brie, Danielle
"L'histoire des phares et de leurs gardiens." Radio program *L'Aventure* produced by CBF, Radio-Canada. Montreal, September 1991.

Bush, Edward F.
"The Canadian Lighthouse." *Canadian Historic Sites: Occasional Papers in Archaeology and History,* no. 9 (Ottawa, 1980), 5–123.

Canada, National Archives
MG 21, Haldimand Papers, vol. 21885.
RG 11, B1 (a) Public Works, vols. 229–35.
RG 12, Transport, vols. 1505, 2126.
RG 42, C1, Marine Branch, vols. 161, 206, 444, 509, 1047.

Canada, Royal Commission on Pilotage
Study of Canadian Pilotage, Gulf and River St. Lawrence. Vol. 4 (1970). Ottawa: Queen's Printer, 1968– . 6 vols.

Canada, Department of Marine and Fisheries
Rules and Instructions for the Guidance of Lightkeepers. Ottawa: Government Printing Bureau, 1912.

Canada, Parliament, House of Commons
Sessional Papers, no. 8, Appendix 37. "Annual Report of the Department of Marine and Fisheries, 1872." Ottawa: Queen's Printer, 1873.

Sessional Papers, no. 21, "Annual Report of the Chief Engineer of the Department of Marine and Fisheries, 1903." Ottawa: Queen's Printer, 1904.

Canada, Department of Transport
General Report of the Commissioner of Public Works, 1867. Ottawa: Hunter Rose and Lemieux, 1868.

Comité des Loisirs de l'Île
Ile Verte, avant-hier au phare … L'Isle-Verte-en-Île: Lévesque-Langlois, 1990.

De Wire, Elinor
"Women of the Lights." *American History Illustrated,* vol. 21, no. 10 (Harrisburg, 1987), 43–49.

Dumoutier, Jean-Paul, and René Gast
Des phares et des hommes. Paris: Éd. Maritimes J.-C. Lallès, 1985.

Faucher de Saint-Maurice
De tribord à bâbord. Montreal: Éd. de l'Aurore, 1975.

Figuier, Louis
"Les phares." In *Les merveilles de la science.* Paris: Jouvet, 1867–70. Vol. 4, 415–528.

Fillmore, Stanley, and R.W. Sandilands
The Chartmakers: The History of Nautical Surveying in Canada. Toronto: N.C. Press, 1983.

France, Archives nationales
Fonds Colonies. Series C[11]A., vol. 104.

Frenette, Pierre
Le phare historique de Pointe-des-Monts et ses gardiens. Sites et villages nord-côtiers, no. 2. Baie-Comeau: Société historique de la Côte-Nord, 1990.

Gignac, Rodrigue
"Hiverner dans un phare." *Cap-aux-Diamants*, no. 24 (Quebec, Winter 1991), 22–25.

Gignac, Rodrigue, and André Ricard
Les phares du Saint-Laurent. Series of thirteen programs produced by CBV Québec. Montreal: Maison de Radio-Canada, Radio Transcript and Product Services, 1978.

Graham, Donald
Lights of the Inside Passage: A History of British Columbia's Lighthouses and Their Keepers. Madeira Park, B.C.: Harbour Publishing, 1986.

Gregory, J.U.
En racontant – Récits de voyages en Floride, au Labrador et sur le fleuve Saint-Laurent. Quebec: Darveau, 1886.

Lasserre, Jean-Claude
Le Saint-Laurent, grande porte de l'Amérique. Montreal: Hurtubise HMH, 1980.

Leclerc, Jean
Le Saint-Laurent et ses pilotes: 1805–1860. Montreal: Leméac, 1991.

O'Farrell, George D.
"Notes on the lighthouses of the Province before the Literary and Historical Society of Quebec." *The Transactions of the Literary and Historical Society of Quebec*, no. 24, Session 1900–1902, 24–36. Quebec: Le Soleil, 1902.

Ouellet, Cécile, and Yvan Chouinard
Autour des îles du Saint-Laurent. Quebec: Ministère des Affaires culturelles, 1984.

Paradis, Jean
"Historique de la station de phare du Cap-de-la-Madeleine." Internal report, Canadian Coast Guard, Laurentian Region. Quebec, n.d.

"Historique de la station de feux d'alignement de Pointe-Noire, P.Q." Internal report, Canadian Coast Guard, Laurentian Region. Quebec, 1984.

Proulx, Gilles
Between France and New France. Toronto: Dundurn Press, 1984.

Quebec. Archives du port de Québec.
Fonds de la Maison de la Trinité de Québec [Holdings of the Trinity House of Quebec] (1805–75)
1.   *Documents reliés* [Bound Volumes]
       A. Minutes Book, vols. 1–14 (1805–75)
       B. Copies of Correspondence, vols. 1–6 (1805–71)
2.   *Documents en feuilles libres* [Unbound Papers]
       III.   Aids to Navigation
       A.   Lighthouses and Lightships 1–25 (1806–70)
               1.5   Correspondence: "Anticosti – Heath Point," 1833–70.
               2.5   Correspondence: "Anticosti – South West Point," 1826–70.
               3.4   Correspondence: "Anticosti – West Point," 1856–68.
               4.3   Correspondence: "Bellechasse," 1862–64, 1870.
               5.5   Correspondence: "Belle-Isle," 1858–64, 1866, 1870.
               6.4   Correspondence: "Biquet," 1844, 1850–54, 1857–64, 1870.
               7.2   Correspondence: "Brandy Pots" (Îles du Pot à l'Eau-de-Vie), 1861–65, 1870.
               8.4   Correspondence: "Cap-des-Rosiers," 1857–64.
               9.2   Correspondence: "Crane Island" (Île aux Grues), 1857, 1860–64.
               10.5   Correspondence: "Father Point" (Pointe au Père), 1860–64.
               11.6   Correspondence: "Forteau ou Pointe-Amour," 1857–64.
               12.3   Correspondence: "Green Island" (Île Verte), 1806–28, 1831–32, 1837, 1850–54, 1857–58, 1860–64.
               13.2   Correspondence: "Grosse-Isle de Kamouraska," 1861–64, 1870.
               14.2   Correspondence: "Pilgrim" (Les Pèlerins), 1862–64, 1869–70.
               15.5   Correspondence: "Pointe-des-Monts," 1825–26, 1829, 1831–32, 1835–36, 1839, 1844, 1849–54, 1857–64, 1870.
               16.1   Correspondence: "Portneuf," 1850–54, 1857–66.
               17.4   Correspondence: "Red Island" (Îlet Rouge), 1831, 1849–54, 1857–58, 1860–64, 1870.
               18.1   Correspondence: "Saint-Antoine," 1854–55, 1860–63.

19.1   Correspondence: "Sainte-Croix," 1843–44, 1850–55, 1857–62.

20.3   Correspondence: "South Pillar" (Pilier Sud), 1842, 1850–55, 1857–58, 1860–64.

21.1   "Dimensions and specifications for a light vessel," 1842, 1856.

21.4   Correspondence: "Light Ship" (at the Haut-Fond de Saint-Roch), 1830–31, 1839, 1841–58, 1860–64.

24.   "Statements of Light Houses," 1846, 1850, 1854, 1857–58, 1861–62, 1864–65, 1868.

25.1   "Admission et conduite des gardiens" (Admission and Conduct of Keepers), *c.* 1850–60.

25.2   "Candidatures au poste de gardien de phare" (Applications for the Position of Lightkeeper), 1827, 1831.

25.3   "Procurations de gardiens" (Keepers' Proxies), forty years between 1811 and 1870.

C.   Dépôts de provisions de l'Ile d'Anticosti (Provision Depots on Anticosti Island), 1 to 5.

E.   Miscellaneous

1   "Rapports d'inspections des phares, bouées, dépôts" (Reports on Inspections of Lighthouses, Bouys, Depots), 1805–19, 1820–53, 1854–75.

2   "Divers phares et dépôts" (Various Lighthouses and Depots), 1815, 1831, 1844, 1850, 1852, 1854, 1857–58, 1861, 1863, 1866–69.

5   "Documentation britannique sur les phares, balises, ports, pilotage" (British Documentation on Lighthouses, Markers, Harbours, Pilotage), 1832, 1835–42.

Rapport de l'archiviste de la province de Québec, 1923–24
Quebec: L.-A. Proulx, 1924.

Report Concerning Canadian Archives, 1905
Ottawa: S.E. Dawson, King's Printer, 1905.

Revue d'histoire du Bas-Saint-Laurent
"Le rapport Taché," vol. 6, no. 1 (Rimouski, January-April 1979).

Rosa, Narcisse
La construction des navires à Québec et ses environs: grèves et naufrages. Québec: L. Brousseau, 1897.

Roy, Pierre-Georges
Le vieux Québec. Vol. 2. Lévis, n.p., 1931.

Smith, William
"The Lighthouse System of Canada." A paper prepared at the request of the Executive Committee of the British Association for the Advancement of Science, read at the Montreal Meeting, 1ˢᵗ Sept. 1884, before Section G, Mechanical Science.

LIST OF PEOPLE INTERVIEWED

FORMER LIGHTKEEPERS
Interviews conducted between April and June 1991

Beck, Réginald, Cap-d'Espoir
Bouchard, Charles-Eugène, Cap de Bon-Désir
Boudreault, Rosaire, Havre-Saint-Pierre
Caron, Luc, Baie-Sainte-Catherine
Carré, Neil, Saint-Siméon
Chiasson, Arthur, Longue-Pointe (Mingan)
Collin, John, Longue-Pointe (Mingan)
Dallaire, Léo, Baic-Sainte-Catherine
Desbien, Yvon, Saint-Patrice
Élément, Yvon, Cap-des-Rosiers
Fergusson, Rémi, Cap-des-Rosiers
Fraser, Charles-Hector, Notre-Dame-de-L'Isle-Verte
Gagnon, Georges-Nil, Tadoussac
Gallienne, Marcel, Sept-Îles
Kavanagh, Robert, Longue-Pointe (Mingan)
Landry, Cyrille, Havre-Saint-Pierre
Lindsay, Charles, Rimouski
Lindsay, Freddy (Mrs.), Rimouski
Ouellet, Léonard, Trois-Pistoles
Poulin, Roger, Tadoussac
Rioux, Jean-Eudes, Rivière-au-Renard
Savard, Fortunat, Saint-Siméon
Simard, Yves, Tadoussac
Therrien, Antoine, Baie-Sainte-Catherine
Therrien, Louis-Joseph, Tadoussac
Therrien, Luc-André, Tadoussac
Therrien, Paul-Étienne, Tadoussac

Thibeault, Maurice, Bic
Thibeault, Patrice, Bic
Trachi, Gordon, Cap-d'Espoir

CANADIAN COAST GUARD, LAURENTIAN REGION

Cloutier, Lise, superintendent of lights (interview, September 25, 1987)
Richard, Gilles, maintenance supervisor, Marine Signals Workshops (interview, July 28, 1994)
Savard, Gilles, superintendent, Navaids (interview, June 1991)